A SWEET WORLD OF
WHITE HOUSE DESSERTS

A SWEET WORLD OF
WHITE
HOUSE
DESSERTS

*From blown-sugar baskets to gingerbread
houses, a pastry chef remembers.*

ROLAND MESNIER
FOREWORD BY GARY WALTERS

WHITE HOUSE HISTORICAL ASSOCIATION
WASHINGTON, D.C.

The WHITE HOUSE HISTORICAL ASSOCIATION is a nonprofit organization, chartered on November 3, 1961, to enhance understanding, appreciation, and enjoyment of the historic White House. Income from the sale of the association's books and guides is returned to the publications program and is used as well to acquire historical furnishings and memorabilia for the White House.

This book has been brought to publication through the generous assistance of the Hon. Walter H. Annenberg White House Publications Fund.

White House Historical Association
740 Jackson Place, N.W.
Washington, D.C. 20006
www.whitehousehistory.org

President: Neil W. Horstman
Vice President of Publications: Marcia Mallet Anderson
Publications Specialist: Nenette Arroyo
Writer: Lauren Chattman
Editorial Consultant: Ann Hofstra Grogg
Color Specialist: Fred Paul
Design: Yacinski Design, LLC
Prepress: Peake DeLancey Printers, Cheverly, Maryland

1st edition
Printed in Italy
9 8 7 6 5 4 3 2

ISBN 978-1-931917-10-0
Library of Congress Control Number 2010934092

I dedicate this book to my entire family,
and especially to my wife Martha,
for all the sacrifices each one of them made so I could
follow my dream and my passion.
Thank you for keeping the fire burning.

— Roland Mesnier

CONTENTS

FOREWORD

WHEN ROLAND MESNIER INFORMED ME IN THE WINTER OF 2003 that he was considering retiring from his position as White House executive pastry chef, I think I must have started to turn blue from lack of oxygen! How do you replace a true artist and consummate professional? Panic was not in my nature, but in this case, I was close to it.

Roland had decided that the time was right for his departure from the White House. He had been here for twenty-five years. Having served in the Executive Residence even longer, I had seen a number of staff members make the same difficult decision to sever their service to the presidency. I do not use the word "sever" lightly, because a position in the President's House is not just a job but a way of life. Most staff members—there are about ninety-five—spend our entire careers here; at one point the average length of service was more than twenty-seven years. Serving the presidency has a special place in our hearts. For those who have this unique opportunity, political affiliation does not enter our minds.

Those of us privileged to serve in the President's House through numerous administrations take pride and satisfaction in knowing that we have done our part to relieve the president and his family from some of the burdens of everyday life and done our best on behalf of the United States. Leaving the President's House thus also means leaving a position you love and a collection of colleagues who have become a close-knit family, having shared in the successes, joys, sorrows, and turmoils of the presidency.

Roland's dedication to his art and the President's House are truly legendary. His aim for the president's foreign guests was to have the desserts he created prompt an emotional response that would honor their heritage in some way. When Roland was informed of an upcoming event, he hit the books. He did research in libraries, bugged the Office of the Curator for information, called the State Department for clues about the likes and dislikes of the future guest, then verified what he learned with the embassy. Finally, his mind on the project whether at the White House or at home, he would plan his creation, frequently drawing designs on paper before starting to work in the Pastry Shop. Roland's artistry was not limited to the highly structured blown- and pulled-sugar or molded chocolate desserts for which he is famous; he was always blending or pairing flavors that others had not thought to bring together. His search for the best ingredients was never ending, and his use of fresh fruits inspired.

Beyond the glorious desserts he created for official and ceremonial events at the White House, Roland also made the daily meals of the president and his family a joy. If there was a holiday, a birthday, an anniversary, or a special family event, he created a unique dessert for the occasion. He always took into account the wishes of the first family, from their dietary preferences to their concerns for calorie counts.

Roland's efforts to produce this book and his generosity in donating the proceeds to the future upkeep of the White House are evidence not only of his unique relationship to the presidency but also of his commitment to the White House and the preservation of its history.

Gary Walters
Chief Usher, The White House, 1986–2007

INTRODUCTION

I T IS EARLY IN THE MORNING ON A COOL DAY IN DECEMBER OF 1979, and I am driving to the White House. I've heard a lot of stories, rumors, and legends about this grand mansion on Pennsylvania Avenue, but I have no personal knowledge of the place and don't have any idea what to expect.

I am famous in the kitchens I have worked in throughout Europe and the United States for my coolness under pressure, so I am surprised at how anxious I feel. Maybe that's why I make several wrong turns before I manage to get myself to the Northwest Gate. As a Secret Service agent approaches to ask me for identification, my heart beats a little faster. He takes my driver's license into the guardhouse, and when he returns he opens the enormous metal gates and instructs me to drive slowly to the North Portico, where I am to park and walk a few steps up to the building. On my way through, I don't fail to notice a row of wrought-iron stars that decorate the gates, and I immediately file away the image, thinking how I'll use similar-looking stars to decorate a dessert.

Before I know it, I am through the door and inside the White House. As I cross the threshold, I think about all the presidents, first ladies, and dignitaries who have walked up the same steps and through the same doorway. I try to take in the furniture, paintings, and fresh flowers as I wait in the entry, but very quickly I am brought back to reality when a staff member taps me on the shoulder and asks me to follow him to the kitchen, where I am to meet the chefs. I remember the real reason for my visit—work!

It is a busy day at the White House, and in the kitchen, because the British prime minister, Margaret Thatcher, is making a state visit. I visit with the chefs and talk to them while they work, and then have a brief talk with the chief usher. Then I am delighted to be invited to the South Lawn, where a ceremony in Mrs. Thatcher's honor is taking place. It is a windy, rainy, cool day, but for me the weather doesn't dim the spectacle of world leaders on the White House lawn. I am in awe. I have no idea how my interview is going, but as far as I'm concerned the opportunity to tour the White House and witness history is satisfying in itself. I think how far I have traveled from my birthplace, a tiny village of 140 people in rural France. It is hard to know how to act in such a palace!

Inside the White House once again, I visit briefly with the food and beverage manager, who leaves me to cool my heels in his office. Impatient because it is a four-hour drive back to my home at the Homestead Hotel in Hot Springs, Virginia, I poke my head out the door and asked someone if I can go home. "Just a little longer," is the reply. After another hour, the phone rings in the office where I'm waiting, and shortly after this I am informed that First Lady Rosalynn Carter is on her way down to meet with me. My heart stops! This isn't in the plan! What am I going to talk about with the first lady? I feel totally unprepared. I tell myself to calm down. I don't really want this job anyway. I am perfectly happy at the Homestead Hotel, with my big pastry shop and capable staff. My wife and son love where we live. Everything is fine!

I'm invited to go outside the office to meet the first lady and her social secretary. Mrs. Carter receives me with a big hug and welcomes me to her home. Her friendliness and sincerity immediately put me at ease, and my panic subsides. Conversation is fun with these two nice ladies. We walk to the Map Room on the Ground Floor of the mansion, and I sit on a beautiful red sofa, with the first lady on my right and the social secretary, Gretchen Poston, on a red chair facing us. Mrs. Carter asks how I enjoyed the ceremony for Prime Minister Thatcher, and laughs out loud when describing how the wind blew her hat off. Then we get down to business, and she asks me all sorts of questions about my work. I show her the photographs I've brought along of some of the desserts I've made at the Homestead and earlier in my career. Our chat takes about 20 minutes, and then she asks me to return to the food and beverage manager's office while she confers with the chief usher. This time, I wait just a few minutes before the usher, the general manager of official and domestic operations in the White House, comes to tell me that Mrs. Carter has agreed to my salary request and wants me to start as soon as possible. I have no idea, at that moment, how my life is about to change.

During the twenty-five years I served as White House pastry chef, I never took for granted the privilege and honor initially bestowed upon me by Mrs. Carter on that chilly afternoon. I had the opportunity to prepare desserts for five presidents, their families, and countless heads of state and VIPs. In gratitude, I tried to create something beautiful and unique for every occasion. I think it is fair to say that I changed people's expectations about White House desserts during my tenure. Because I never repeated myself, there was always great anticipation surrounding what I'd come up with next. Far from feeling pressure, I loved the challenge and strived with each of my creations to bring great pleasure to all the guests I served.

This book is a record of some of the most celebrated and interesting desserts I created at the White House. It is my legacy, and I am so proud to share it with you. It is also a thank-you note to America and to the White House, a sanctuary where I was allowed to exercise my skill and creativity to the fullest, and realize every single professional ambition I ever had, and some I never knew I had. Proceeds from the sale of this book will contribute to the preservation and upkeep of this very special house.

It was extremely difficult to choose which desserts to feature. Going through my vast collection of sketches, notes, photographs, and menus brought back so many wonderful memories of every presidential administration and so many special occasions, from Chelsea Clinton's birthday parties with school friends to a grand dinner in honor of Queen Elizabeth II. The desserts that appear in the following pages are a fair representation of what came out of the White House pastry kitchen during my tenure. There are desserts inspired by the flavors of a particular place (the coffee-themed Best of Kenya State Dinner dessert), examples of the delicate sugar work in which I took so much pride (the sugar tulip baskets served at the State Dinner in honor of Queen Beatrix of the Netherlands), and desserts representing a president's favorite pastime (chocolate cookies shaped into baseball gloves, complete with *meringue* baseballs for a Baseball Hall of Fame Luncheon). I loved working for each and every president and first lady, but I did create more desserts for some than for others, and that is reflected in the contents. I served the Carter administration for only a year, so there are relatively few Carter-era desserts here. Some administrations entertained more than others. The Reagan White House had a particularly busy social calendar, as did the Clinton White House. Both Bush administrations were comparatively quiet.

With my final choices, I have tried to give a broad view of White House desserts over a quarter century. And looking back, I see that these desserts are a reflection of the important people and events of the period. I was in the unique position of witnessing American history from the pastry kitchen, and I chronicled what I saw in flour and butter and sugar. But when I worked, I wasn't thinking of history. I had only one goal in mind: pleasing the guest of honor

Chief Usher Gary Walters presents Pastry Chef Roland Mesnier with his workbench as a gift upon his retirement from the White House in a small celebration attended by President and Mrs. George W. Bush and many of the chef's White House colleagues. A plaque denoting his tenure in the position was specially made for the piece.

with a tailor-made dessert. To hear applause coming from the dining room as my desserts were carried in, or to be told by the White House butlers that a particular creation had actually brought a tear to the eye of a head of state, or to be thanked personally by the president or first lady for a job well done—these were the moments I lived for and what drove me to work long hours in a continuing effort to amaze and delight. When I look through this collection, I see both the big picture and remember every small but touching moment. I am amazed at what I was able to imagine and to produce with my own two hands, when given the inspiration and opportunity. I hope you will be amazed, too.

There are no recipes included here, because each of these desserts was a one-time-only creation, made of many separate components and extremely complicated to put together. If you'd like a taste of what I served at the White House, you might take a look at the cookbooks I've written in the years since I've retired. Both *Dessert University* and *Basic to Beautiful Cakes* include many recipes for simpler versions of some of the spectacular creations you will see on the following pages.

On July 30, 2004, my last day arrived—a very bittersweet day—and I hated to say goodbye to the Bush family and all my friends. I decided it would be just a regular day of work for me as I had had a lot of time to think about my departure since I gave six months' notice. On that day I came to work at the regular time; before leaving at 3:00 p.m. I cleaned all the dishes and turned out the light for the last time. As I was coming downstairs from the Pastry Shop I couldn't find anyone—strange! As I turned into the long corridor leading me outside I was deeply moved to see that all the staff had lined up to bid me farewell.

STATE OCCASIONS

*President Carter meets with German Chancellor Helmut Schmidt in the Oval Office,
following the arrival ceremony for the State Visit.*

ERY EARLY IN MY CAREER (when just 18) I was apprenticed to a pastry chef in Germany, and I developed a good knowledge of German tastes and classic German dessert-making. I called on that knowledge when designing a dessert for the State Dinner in honor of Chancellor Helmut Schmidt of Germany, making a fluffy rice pudding by folding some *meringue* and whipped cream, with a small amount of gelatin, into the creamy rice and candied fruit. The mixture was poured into ring molds and chilled overnight. Before the dinner, I unmolded the rice puddings and decorated them with chocolate and different colored jellies. Then I placed poached pears all around each ring. The centers were filled with strawberries, and vanilla sauce was served on the side.

I took care to match the *petits fours* to the occasion. Not only did I match the flowers on top of the white chocolates with those on the puddings, but I shaped butter cookie dough into pretzel shapes, in a nod to our guest's homeland.

Pears Imperatrice and Petits Fours

Dinner, March 5, 1980

NEW ORLEANS GUMBO
ALMADEN *Dry Sherry*

ROAST TENDERLOIN OF BEEF

DAUPHIN POTATOES
SPINACH SOUFFLÉ

MIRASSOU *Gamay Beaujolais*

PEARS IMPERATRICE
SAUCE SABAYON

SCHRAMSBERG *Blanc de Blancs*

DEMITASSE

*The Guarneri String Quartet, an American ensemble, performs
for guests at the State Dinner.*

I DON'T THINK I EVER WITNESSED such a production, before or since, as the preparation for the State Dinner for Prime Minister Menachem Begin of Israel. First of all, the kitchen had to be certified as kosher before any food could be brought in. This involved cleansing the utensils, stainless steel prep tables, and ovens with a special torch. Work surfaces that could not be burned had to be covered with aluminum foil. All of the china and silverware had to be boiled in a giant kettle, which itself had been burned with the torch.

All food preparation was supervised by a rabbi who had been sent to us specially for the task. The dinner was to be dairy-free, including my dessert, an orange *sorbet* cake. Every time I turned around, there was the rabbi, watching to make sure that the ingredients going into my cake were kosher. There was no problem with the *génoise* layers, which I baked at the White House. He also approved the dairy-free whipped topping that was to frost the cake and the caramel-dipped orange segments that were to decorate it. But since my ice cream machine had churned many batches of dairy-rich ice cream and couldn't be boiled or cleansed with the torch, the rabbi insisted that I make the *sorbet*—just orange juice and sugar—in a brand-new machine. I knew from a friend that Jean-Louis, a restaurant at the Watergate Hotel, had just unpacked a new ice cream freezer and hadn't yet used it, so I high-tailed it over there to make my *sorbet*, packed it in ice, and rushed back to the White House.

After the dinner, the White House butler reported the review: Prime Minister Begin had said the cake was the best kosher dessert he had ever tasted. Receiving this praise made everything—the extra help from the rabbi, the trip to and from the Watergate—seem like small sacrifices.

Orange Sherbet Cake

Dinner, April 15, 1980

COLD COLUMBIAN RIVER SALMON
SAUCE VERTE
SESAME STICKS

ROAST DUCKLING WITH
  GLAZED PEACHES AND WILD RICE
FRESH ASPARAGUS

MIXED GREEN SALAD

FROZEN ORANGE SHERBET CAKE
GRAND MARNIER SAUCE

President Carter speaks at the luncheon for King Baudouin,
who is seated to his left and next to First Lady Rosalynn Carter. Queen Fabiola, to the president's right,
was also honored. The table is decorated with dogwood flowers.

*Y*HIS IS ONE OF THE FIRST desserts I made as White House pastry chef, for a luncheon in honor of King Baudouin of Belgium. The luncheon took place in the East Room, the largest State Room in the White House. The long banquet table was set with shining vermeil and decorated with dogwood flowers. First Lady Rosalynn Carter and her social secretary, Gretchen Poston, often ordered flowers from florists across the country to show off the best of the United States at these events. On the menu were cold lobster and medaillons of veal. At this early stage in my job, I didn't keep many records or take many photographs of my work, uncertain and nervous as I was about how everything was going. But this dessert stood out to me for its simple beauty and the way it matched the table and the food. Although I would later make more elaborately decorated desserts, I would always try for a similar harmony of elements in everything I brought to the table.

Coconut Ice Cream
in Hibiscus Flower Shell

Luncheon, April 22, 1980

COLD LOBSTER
SAUCE RÉMOULADE
GOLDEN TWISTS

MEDAILLONS OF VEAL
GARDEN VEGETABLES

COCONUT ICE CREAM IN
  HIBISCUS SHELL
PETITS FOURS

DEMITASSE

BEAULIEU VINEYARD *Pinot Chardonnay*
SIMI ROSÉ *Cabernet Sauvignon*
KORBEL *Natural Champagne*

President and Mrs. Reagan welcome the guests of honor, King Juan Carlos I and Queen Sofia, on the North Portico of the White House.

INCE SPAIN IS WELL KNOWN for its beautiful citrus fruits, this is the angle I chose when designing desserts for two State Dinners for Spain. The first occasion was in the fall of 1981, when in celebration of the autumn, I made a pear sorbet and presented it in an elaborate pulled-sugar basket decorated with blown-sugar pears.

For the second occasion during the William J. Clinton Administration, I made orange *sorbet* and molded it in the shape of the oranges. Hidden inside each orange was a portion of Grand Marnier *mousse* with some crunchy *nougat*. But I didn't stop there. I then made clementine *sorbet*, molded it in the shape of clementines, and filled each one with vanilla *mousse* and candied ginger. The lemon *sorbet* got a similar treatment, with mango *mousse* and crispy *meringue*. Lime *sorbet* concealed honey *mousse* and caramelized pecans. So beautiful and so delicious!

As always, I took as much care constructing the containers as I did making the *sorbet* fruits. The boxes holding each topiary (pictured on page 142), were molded from white chocolate and displayed the emblem of the king on all four sides. On each corner of each box was a little vase made of white chocolate and filled with *marzipan* roses. A dowel made of chocolate and fixed to the bottom of each box with more chocolate served to hold the *sorbet* fruits in place. Just before serving, I piped a little bit of whipped cream between the fruits, to hold more *marzipan* roses and crystallized violets. Then I decorated each platter with fresh kumquats and raspberries. I also piped a little chocolate onto the top of the chocolate dowel and glued a long pulled-sugar orange blossom branch to the top of the dessert, giving it spectacular height. A glazed kumquat sauce accompanied the platters, as did caramel walnut candy and raspberry-ginger butter cookies. Over the top? Perhaps, but I wouldn't have been satisfied otherwise!

Fantasy of Pear Sorbet
in a Sugar Basket

Dinner, October 13, 1981

COLD COLUMBIA RIVER SALMON
  EN GELÉE
DILL SAUCE

SUPRÊME OF CHICKEN VÉRONIQUE
WILD RICE AMANDINE
BRAISED ENDIVE

BIBB LETTUCE SALAD
GOURMANDISE CHEESE WITH WALNUTS

FANTAISIE OF PEAR SORBET IN A BASKET
APRICOT SLICES

GRGICH HILLS *Chardonnay 1979*
CHALONE VINEYARD *Pinot Noir, Vin Gris 1980*
SCHRAMSBERG *Crémant Demi-sec 1979*

*President Reagan speaks in the State Dining Room during the State Dinner
for Queen Beatrix and Prince Claus of the Netherlands.*

I WAS STILL NEW AT MY JOB when the Reagan administration arrived at the White House. We were warned ahead of time that the new president and first lady intended to entertain in a more serious way than the rather laid-back Carters. From Day One, First Lady Nancy Reagan made it clear that everything coming from the kitchen had to meet her incredibly high standards. She had to approve everything personally, and there was no gray area. She either liked what you showed her or didn't, and if she didn't you had to go back to work to come up with something that would meet her expectations.

I absolutely loved working for her! Although it was sometimes very stressful, trying to please her was the best way I knew to challenge and surpass myself as a pastry chef. Any success I had at the White House came from my early experiences of reaching for the stars every single time I made something for the president and first lady.

During the first year of the Reagan administration, I spent several weeks preparing sample desserts for a State Dinner to be held in honor of the queen of the Netherlands and Prince Claus. I went up to the private quarters three times with a new dessert, and each time Mrs. Reagan rejected the prototype I had worked up. "It's just not clicking for me, Roland," she would say. "Keep trying. I'll know it when I see it." It wasn't her habit to give me her own ideas, but she

could see I was frustrated, and at the third tasting she suggested I base my next attempt on the idea of a basket of tulips made of pulled sugar and sent me back to the kitchen.

Sugar work is one of my specialties, but sugar baskets and flowers are among the most time-consuming and difficult of sugar decorations. It took me the better part of a day to make an exquisitely detailed basket with three tulips. I filled it with the fat-free *sorbets* that Mrs. Reagan preferred to ice cream, and I crossed my fingers. When the first lady came into the pastry kitchen to check my progress, she gave me the go-ahead. I should have been happy, but my heart sank. It had taken so long to find the right dessert that there were just two days left until the dinner. "But Mrs. Reagan! I only have two days!" I exclaimed in a panicked voice. "Two days and two nights," she corrected me.

In those days I had no assistant. So I worked virtually nonstop all by myself for the next 48 hours to produce fifteen baskets, forty-five tulips, and the fresh fruit *sorbets* for the dessert, finishing just as the dinner was beginning. I decided to stay to see how they were received. The White House butler rushed back to the pastry kitchen after dessert was served to report that the queen was delighted with the tribute to her country, and the president and first lady happily accepted her compliments. I was joyful that I had met Mrs. Reagan's expectations.

Sugar Tulip Baskets
with Orange Sherbet

Dinner, April 19, 1982

POACHED FILET OF POMPANO BEATRIX
FLEURONS

ROAST BEEF TENDERLOIN HEARTS
SAUCE BÉARNAISE
SOUFFLÉ POTATOES
ARTICHOKES PRINTANIÈRE

BIBB LETTUCE SALAD
BRIE CHEESE—FINES HERBES

SUGAR TULIP BASKET
  WITH ORANGE SORBET
PETITS FOURS

TREFETHEN *Chardonnay 1979*
JORDAN *Cabernet Sauvignon 1976*
SCHRAMSBERG *Crémant Demi-sec 1979*

*The petit four tray includes eight types of cookies
and a pulled-sugar flower basket.*

WHEN A SPECIAL EVENT was scheduled for early December, I always got a little anxious. To prepare for the holiday season, during which we fed literally thousands of guests at the White House, I had to have about 120,000 servings of cake and cookies ready by December 1. But I was not about to let this stop me from preparing a very special, very royal dessert for King Birendra and Queen Aishwarya of Nepal at the same time.

To deliver something different from the holiday fare everyone would be seeing for the next few weeks, I decided to look ahead to spring. I would serve some deliciously light mango, lemon, and raspberry *sorbets*, along with a Grand Marnier *parfait*. The presentation would be key. I knew I wanted to include some pulled-sugar cherry blossoms and spring flowers. But I needed something else to bring these elements into focus. I came up with the idea of the swan, a regal bird famous for its spring migration. It was perfect.

First, I made a large blown-sugar swan with his beak reaching for some sugar cherry blossoms. I filled the swan with Grand Marnier *parfait*. I molded the *sorbet* into roses, then arranged them so they cascaded down the swan's fully open wing. Pulled-sugar tulips, crocuses, daffodils, and primroses surrounding the swan were like a lakeside spring flower garden. Cattails and long leaves enhanced the impression of a beautiful country setting. I always tried to incorporate fresh fruit into my desserts, and in this case melon balls and fresh raspberries further beautified the platter.

I wanted a *petit four* tray that wouldn't pale in comparison, so in addition to eight different types of cookies, each tray included a sugar basket with its own pulled-sugar spring flowers. People who know me recognize my love of gardening, which knows no bounds, when they look at these pictures. When it comes to flowers, whether real or of pulled sugar and *sorbet*, I can never have enough!

Fantasy of Spring Sorbets

Dinner, December 7, 1983

VEGETABLE PÂTÉ
TOMATO COULIS
SESAME SEED TWISTS

SADDLE OF LAMB FARCI
WILD RICE WITH MUSHROOMS
BRAISED CELERY AU GRATIN

SPINACH AND WATER CHESTNUT SALAD
BRIE CHEESE

SUGAR SWAN WITH SORBET AND FRUIT
PETITS FOURS

TREFETHEN *Chardonnay 1980*
JORDAN *Cabernet Sauvignon 1979*
KORBEL *Blanc de Noir*

The violinist Isaac Stern performs in the East Room after dinner.

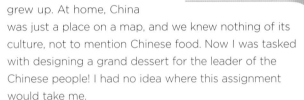

WHEN I WAS GIVEN the assignment of creating a dessert for a dinner in honor of the premier of China, Zhao Zhiyang, I couldn't help but think of how far I had come from the little village of Bonnay in France where I grew up. At home, China was just a place on a map, and we knew nothing of its culture, not to mention Chinese food. Now I was tasked with designing a grand dessert for the leader of the Chinese people! I had no idea where this assignment would take me.

One of the most enjoyable and interesting parts of my job was researching the culture and food of an unfamiliar country in order to come up with something appropriate and pleasing to our foreign guests. Before this particular dinner, I spent many hours in bookstores and at the library, reading about China and looking at pictures of Chinese art and architecture, to get an idea of what might catch the premier's eye. Then I looked at many Chinese cookbooks to learn about Chinese desserts.

I'll confess that I was a little discouraged by what I found. It seemed that aside from melon and a few simple custards, the Chinese didn't really enjoy dessert at all! I reminded myself of all of the pictures of exotic fruits I had seen not only in the cookbooks but in the art books I had paged through. Pomegranates and lychees were well represented, so I decided to focus on these fruits. I'd make a pomegranate *sorbet* with fresh lychees, mixing in some raspberries for color and garnishing the dessert with *sabayon*, a French sauce that would add richness to the fruit.

Once I determined the components of the dessert, I had to come up with a beautiful and original way to present them. Before doing anything, I consulted with the State Department to make sure that the dessert was sensitive to Chinese culture. I learned, for example, that white flowers were out, since in China they are only used at funerals. Two images from my research—the phoenix and the small boat known as a junk—had captured my imagination. Neither was off-limits. I'd make a junk out of sugar to hold the dessert, and a phoenix to garnish it.

To create a prototype for Mrs. Reagan (all State Dinner desserts during the Reagan years were approved by the first lady well in advance of the event), I carved the boat out of a thick piece of wood. I covered my wooden boat with plastic wrap, then molded warm pieces of pulled sugar around it to create the shape in an edible form. Once the sugar pieces hardened, I removed them from my model and reassembled them on their own. Then, consulting a Chinese picture of a phoenix, I made one from blown sugar. I sat it on a sugar branch, covered with Chinese plum blossoms and leaves. Its long feathers swept around the side of the vessel, which was now ready to be filled with the *sorbet* and fruit and presented to the first lady. I was thrilled when she gave me the go-ahead.

Not so thrilled was my assistant pastry chef, who was in charge of extracting the juice from dozens of pomegranates, a difficult job. For months and years afterward, if I ever wanted to tease or scare her, I'd tell her that I'd ordered two cases of pomegranates for her to prep!

Pomegranate Sorbet
with Lychees and Raspberries

Dinner, January 10, 1984

POACHED TURBOT
SAUCE AURORA
SESAME SEED TWISTS

BEEF FARCI EN CROÛTE
TRUFFLE SAUCE
POTATOES SOUFFLÉ
CARROT RING

GARDEN GREEN SALAD WITH WALNUTS

POMEGRANATE SORBET WITH
  FRESH FRUIT
PETITS FOURS SEC

PINE RIDGE *Chardonnay 1981*
SILVER OAK *Cabernet Sauvignon 1978*
SCHRAMSBERG *Crémant Demi-sec 1981*

*Mexican President Miguel de la Madrid, seated beside First Lady Nancy Reagan,
helps himself to the Tequila Mousse.*

*I*N THE 1970s, before I worked at the
White House, I had the wonderful
experience of helping to open the
Acapulco Princess, at the time one of
the world's most spectacular hotels.
The hotel's owner, D. K. Ludwig, was reportedly the
richest man in the world. The opening night was like a
Hollywood production. The Dom Pérignon flowed, and
the largest *mariachi* band ever assembled strolled
throughout the lobby and the grounds, serenading
guests with traditional Mexican songs. To drum up
American business, Mr. Ludwig had invited every sitting
U.S. governor. The majority took him up on the offer.

Living in Acapulco was a wonderful experience.
During that time, I fell in love with the exotic fruits and
spices used in Mexican cooking and utilized many of
them in the desserts I designed and served at the hotel.
Years later at the White House, I was excited to draw on
this experience when crafting a dessert for a State
Dinner honoring Mexican President Miguel de la Madrid.

A tequila *mousse* accompanied by kiwi and coconut
sorbet would be just right, I thought. Tequila happens to
go great with acidic flavors, as anyone who's had a mar-
garita made with fresh lime juice can tell you. As for
presentation, I molded the *sorbet* into hollow cactus
shapes (I had chosen the kiwi not only for its acidity, but
because I thought its color would be great for this pur-
pose), filled the cacti with the tequila *mousse*, and garnished them with pulled-sugar cactus flowers and
pulled-sugar spines. Then each platter was decorated
with some long-stemmed strawberries and shredded
coconut.

In this photo, President de la Madrid and Mrs.
Reagan are about to try my creation. Note that the
service is what we call "Russian," meaning that instead
of serving individual plated desserts, the White House
butlers offer platters of food to guests, who help themselves. This type of service, I believe, reminds our
guests that they aren't eating at a hotel or restaurant,
but in a home.

Tequila Mousse
with Kiwi and Coconut Sorbet

Dinner, May 15, 1984

LOBSTER IN PORT JELLY
RÉMOULADE SAUCE
PITA BREAD

TOURNEDOS WITH TRUFFLE SAUCE
SPRING POTATOES
CARROT RING AND GREEN PEAS

BIBB LETTUCE AND RADICCHIO SALAD
BEL PAESE CHEESE

COCONUT SORBET
GALLETAS

FRANCISCAN *Chardonnay Estate 1982*
BUENA VISTA *Pinot Noir Special Selection 1981*
SCHRAMSBERG *Crémant Demi-sec 1981*

*President Reagan touches the trunk of a baby elephant,
a gift from President Junius R. Jayewardene of Sri Lanka.*

ECAUSE THIS DINNER TOOK PLACE during cherry season, I was determined to use fresh cherries in the dessert. In my original design, I molded lime *sorbet* and coconut ice cream into the shape of asparagus stalks and filled this crown-like container with pitted cherries. As soon as Mrs. Reagan saw it she shot it down. She didn't want the cherries to roll into the guests' laps as they helped themselves to the *sorbet*. So it was back to the drawing board. Next I folded the pitted cherries into a thick red currant jelly to hold them together, and on the second try I got the thumbs up. A yellow, white, and green sugar ribbon bow decorated the final dessert, along with fresh mandarin orange segments dipped into caramel. Everything was arranged on a *nougat* platter.

I wasn't at all jealous when a special presentation by President Jayewardene to President Reagan eclipsed talk of dessert that night. It is common for gifts to be exchanged between the two leaders during State Visits and then sent to museums or libraries for the public to enjoy. But on this visit, President Reagan received one of the most memorable gifts on record: a beautiful baby elephant from an elephant orphanage in the hill country of Sri Lanka! Since the elephant is both the symbol of the Sri Lankan presidency and of the Republican Party, she was particularly appropriate. Her name was Jayathu, which means "victory," and she immediately became the talk of the town. She was sent to the National Zoo, where she had a comfortable home and where I went to visit her many times, each time remembering this State Dinner.

Nougat Glacé with Fresh Cherries
and Coconut Ice Cream Asparagus

Dinner, June 18, 1984

POACHED SALMON AND
  CUCUMBER MOUSSE
RED CAVIAR SAUCE
MELBA TOAST

SUPRÊME OF CORNISH HEN WITH
  BLACK CHERRIES
SAUTÉED RICE
GARDEN BEANS AND WHITE TURNIPS

BELGIAN ENDIVE AND FIELD SALAD
BRIE CHEESE

NOUGAT GLACÉ
CARAMEL OR RASPBERRY SAUCE
PETITS FOURS SEC

PAULSEN *Muscat Canelli 1983*
MATANZAS CREEK *Chardonnay 1981*
KORBEL *Blanc de Noirs*

31

Pulled-sugar baskets were created for Queen Sirikit's 1985 visit to the White House. For her 2002 visit, sugar-baskets were again the centerpiece of the dessert, this time filled with guava and mango sorbet "roses" and sugar orchids.

QUEEN SIRIKIT OF THAILAND made several visits to the White House over the years, so I had several opportunities to create desserts for her. On one memorable visit she was honored at a small black-tie dinner hosted by President and Mrs. Reagan. The dinner, for about thirty, was served on the Reagan china in the President's Dining Room. For dessert, I made pulled-sugar baskets woven in a characteristic Thai shape and filled each one with an assortment of fruit *sorbets*. This is one of my favorite White House photos, because it shows President Reagan digging in with enthusiasm as the queen looks on with a big smile. He was such a connoisseur and admirer of my sugar work, and he loved sweets.

In October 2002, the charming queen returned to Washington, this time as a guest of President and Mrs. George W. Bush. The luncheon was an intimate gathering, with a small group of carefully selected guests. I wanted to make a dainty dessert appropriate for the occasion, using the flavors of Thailand. This time I shaped guava and mango *sorbet* into beautiful roses and presented them in a pulled-sugar basket decorated with pastel-colored sugar orchids. The platter was decorated with blackberries, raspberries, and fresh lychees, with kiwi leaves all around. Delicate cookies shaped like water lilies were passed separately. I hope that the beauty and delicacy of the dessert reflected those same qualities that were so apparent in the queen.

Thai Dessert Baskets

Dinner, March 11, 1985

GOLDEN CONSOMMÉ
SHRIMP AND DILL RONDELLES

HONEY CHICKEN WITH GINGER
BASIL RICE TIMBALE
BOUQUETS OF VEGETABLES

MANDARIN SPINACH SALAD
POPPY SEED DRESSING

THAI BASKETS OF FRUIT SORBET
MANGO AND RASPBERRY SAUCES

TREFETHEN *White Riesling 1982*
SANFORD *Pinot Noir Vin Gris 1983*
SCHRAMSBERG *Crémant Demi-sec 1980*

*President and Mrs. Reagan visit with Prince Charles and Princess Diana
in the West Sitting Hall of the White House.*

WHEN THE PRINCE AND PRINCESS OF WALES were scheduled to visit the White House in November 1985, Mrs. Reagan and the entire kitchen staff were determined to pull out all of the stops. Would we be able to produce a dinner as fresh, beautiful, and charming as the young Princess Diana? We were all inspired and challenged. Mrs. Reagan had heard that the princess was especially fond of peaches, so we started there. The very pretty and feminine colors of the fruit dictated her choice of table linens and flowers. Every table would have a big glass bowl filled with peach-colored roses.

When it came to the dessert, I had to figure out how to bring out the flavor of the peaches, honor the prince and princess, and match my dessert to the colors of the room. *Sorbet* made from ripe southern peaches would capture the sweetness and perfume of the fruit. I molded the *sorbet* into peach shapes with a chocolate center made to look like the stone of the fruit. Next, I made the white chocolate baskets to hold the *sorbet* peaches. As a final garnish, I made several dozen *marzipan* roses, all the exact color of the flowers that had been ordered for the tables. The roses would sit inside the baskets, scattered among the *sorbet* peaches. Pale yellow Champagne sauce, served in bowls on the side, would accompany each basket.

At a certain point in the design process, I realized that I was making the dessert without a thought for the prince. Ted Graber, Mrs. Reagan's interior designer and good friend, suggested I take the three white plumes from the prince's coat of arms and use them as a decoration for the top of the sugar basket. Although I could make many delicate shapes with blown sugar, I was having a hard time making featherweight plumes by this method. Mrs. Reagan wanted the right kind of plumes very badly, so I knew I'd have to find another way. I went to the White House Carpentry Shop and carved the right-sized plume shapes from pieces of wood. I took my molds back to the kitchen, lined them with plastic wrap, and pressed warm pulled sugar into the molds. Then I laid another piece of plastic wrap over the sugar and pressed until the sugar was very thin. I had just what I wanted, very fine feathers with exquisite detail on both sides. Mr. Graber and Mrs. Reagan approved the new version that night, and the next day I started manufacturing them for the dinner.

Like everyone else who worked at the White House, I was desperate to get a glimpse of the princess, so I began to plot ways to see her. She was taking tea with Mrs. Reagan the day before the dinner and I, knowing that she would be arriving at the White House at a certain time, strategically positioned myself near the East Wing, pretending to pick some mint. There was a perfect view of the driveway from my mint patch, and I looked up when I heard her car pulling up to the door. When I returned with my mint, I was able to report to the rest of the kitchen staff that she was just as beautiful as we had heard.

The State Dinner itself was magical, and I think the dessert achieved the elegance Mrs. Reagan insisted upon. I was proud to serve it on the Reagan china. Every member of the White House staff had come together to make this celebration perfect, and 1600 Pennsylvania Avenue never looked better!

Peach Sorbet Basket
with Champagne Sauce and Petits Fours

Dinner, November 9, 1985

LOBSTER MOUSSELINE WITH
  MARYLAND CRAB
HORSERADISH SAUCE

GLAZED CHICKEN CAPSICUM
BROWN RICE
GARDEN VEGETABLES

JiCAMA SALAD
HERBED CHEESE
CROUTONS

PEACH SORBET BASKET
CHAMPAGNE SAUCE
PETITS FOURS

QUAIL RIDGE *Chardonnay 1981*
CONN CREEK *Cabernet Sauvignon 1979*
SCHRAMSBERG *Cuvée de Pinot 1982*

The State Dining Room during the State Dinner for the Prince and Princess of Wales, 1985

*A White House butler presents the Orange Surprise dessert to First Lady Nancy Reagan and
Prime Minister Yasuhiro Nakasone during the State Dinner for Japan.*

MRS. REAGAN undoubtedly put her stamp on White House entertaining while she was first lady, for she influenced the way food was prepared and presented well beyond the Reagan years. From Day One of her tenure, it was understood that she would have to approve every menu item for every special luncheon and dinner in advance of the event. So we set up elaborate tastings for her, which we called "tryouts," preparing an entire meal for the eight to ten people she would bring with her to the dining room for their opinions. She had extremely high standards. The food had to be beautiful and colorful—nothing gray. It had to be artistically displayed, but recognizable; she didn't want people to wonder what they were eating. Elegance was the watchword. She was partial to platter service, also called "Russian service." But she insisted that the food be very lightly sauced, so there would be no danger that guests would stain their clothes when they helped themselves. She truly thought of everything.

For the tryout, the table would be set as if for the meal, wines would be sampled, and the food would be served as planned. The executive chef, the *maître d'*, and I would wait in the kitchen until the dishes were cleared, and then the first lady, accompanied by the White House decorator, Ted Graber, would come to see us and the critique would begin. She would proceed from first course to dessert, directing us to make changes as she went. We took Polaroid photos and notes during these sessions so there would be no excuse for mistakes at the luncheon or dinner itself.

I absolutely loved working this way. The first lady's high standards inspired me to strive for perfection. This particular dessert, created for Prime Minister Yasuhiro Nakasone of Japan and his wife Tsutako Nakasone is one I'm really proud of for its beauty and intricacy. I made oversized blown-sugar oranges. Each one was about the size of a cantaloupe. Then I carefully removed the tops of the oranges with a special saw. The oranges were frozen and then sprayed with orange-colored chocolate, so their surfaces resembled the peel of a real orange. They were filled with a *gianduja mousse* mixed with caramelized chocolate-almond clusters, and then the *mousse* was topped with orange *sorbet*. Fresh orange segments and peel garnished the platter.

I treasure this photo of Mrs. Reagan serving the dessert, with the prime minister looking on. The butler told me that Mr. Nakasone asked Mrs. Reagan, "Where do you grow such big oranges?" and she replied, "Only in California!"

Orange Surprise

Dinner, April 30, 1987

COLUMBIA RIVER SMOKED SALMON
HORSERADISH SAUCE
FENNEL TWISTS

CHAMPAGNE CHICKEN TARRAGON
WILD RICE IN TURNIPS
EARLY SPRING ZUCCHINI

FIELD SALAD WITH WALNUT DRESSING
BEL PAESE CHEESE
MELBA TOAST

ORANGE SURPRISE
PETITS FOURS SEC

JORDAN *Chardonnay 1984*
SCHUG CELLARS *Pinot Noir 1984*
CHÂTEAU ST. JEAN *1983*

*President Reagan dines with Soviet General Secretary Mikhail Gorbachev and Raisa
Gorbachev in the State Dining Room in 1987.*

THE INCREASINGLY WARM relationship between the general secretary and the president had generated a lot of interest in the press. The world was watching, so even for the White House this was a high-profile event. When Mikhail Gorbachev arrived in Washington, it was clear that he was well liked. I remember the mobs that surrounded him, hoping to shake his hand, when he got out of his car on Wisconsin Avenue.

As always, while referring to a nation's culture I was careful to avoid political or religious references for fear of giving offense or creating a misunderstanding. I designed the dessert to exhibit some Russian flair, starting with the chocolate base, which had a pattern borrowed from the parquet floor in the Kremlin. Two sugar baskets with white and green pulled-sugar ribbons held fresh raspberries, a delicacy in Russia—just as caviar is a delicacy in the United States. In the center of the platter was a sphere of honey vanilla ice cream

filled with a tea *parfait,* honey and tea being two very popular flavors in Russia. I molded the small chocolate candies that you can see in front of the ice cream to resemble the onion domes of the Kremlin. Acorn-shaped *meringue* cookies filled with vodka jam completed the presentation.

Following the State Dinner, President Reagan and General Secretary Gorbachev traveled to Camp David. Some of the kitchen staff, including myself, went along to prepare the luncheon. In the late morning I stepped out of the kitchen to get a breath of fresh air, and just steps away I saw the two leaders strolling across the grass in quiet conversation. They were headed right toward me. Protocol demanded that I retreat, since the staff was not supposed to be seen or heard. But like so many other Americans I wanted to shake the Russian leader's hand so badly! After a brief inner struggle I went back to the kitchen, sorry not to have been able to exchange words with the general secretary or express my admiration.

Honey Vanilla Ice Cream
with Russian Tea Parfait

Dinner, December 8, 1987

COLUMBIA RIVER SALMON &
  LOBSTER MEDALLIONS EN GELÉE
CAVIAR SAUCE
FENNEL SEED TWISTS

LOIN OF VEAL WITH WILD MUSHROOMS
CHAMPAGNE SAUCE
TARRAGON TOMATOES
CORN TURBAN

MEDLEY OF GARDEN GREENS
BRIE CHEESE WITH CRUSHED WALNUTS
VINEGAR & AVOCADO OIL DRESSING

TEA SORBET IN HONEY ICE CREAM

JORDAN *Chardonnay 1984*
STAGS' LEAP *Cabernet Sauvignon Lot 2 1978*
IRON HORSE *Brut Summit Cuvée 1984*

The Neptune Fountain in front of the Drottningholm Palace west of Stockholm is one of many Swedish fountains that inspired the dessert served at the dinner honoring King Carl XVI Gustav and Queen Silvia.

OR THIS INTIMATE OCCASION, a dinner for forty in the President's Dining Room, I wanted to create something very grand and royal. I had seen photos of the many fountains that beautify Stockholm, so I decided to make the base of the dessert look like a fountain. The dolphins aren't copied from a particular Swedish monument, but came from my imagination. You can see them spouting green pulled sugar into white chocolate basins that I filled with green-colored corn syrup. The basins are surrounded by mounds of beautiful raspberries. A heavy chocolate dowel is holding a chocolate plate above the dolphins. On the plate is the dessert itself—thin slices of cantaloupe filled with a delicate fresh apricot *mousse*. *Nougat barquettes* filled with raspberry and kiwi *sorbets* surround the *mousse*. Each one is topped with a white chocolate crown. Garnishing the mousse is a small white chocolate fountain with more pulled sugar, to match the dolphins below.

When I previewed the dessert for Mrs. Reagan, she told me I had outdone myself and that it was gorgeous. I felt great! I threw myself into preparing the desserts I needed for the real dinner and delighted in creating beautiful *petit four* trays with hand-decorated butterfly cookies, chocolate truffles, and Florentine squares, each tray decorated with sugar crocuses and leaves to celebrate the season.

Fresh Fruit Bavarian

Dinner, April 11, 1988

LOBSTER BISQUE WITH
  CRABMEAT RAVIOLI
CAVIAR RISSOLES

MEDALLION OF DELAWARE
  LAMB EN CROÛTE
SAUCE PALOISE
POTATO NEST WITH SPRING
  VEGETABLES
FRESH ASPARAGUS

WATERCRESS, MUSHROOM AND
  ENDIVE SALAD
RASPBERRY VINAIGRETTE

FRESH FRUIT BAVARIAN
ASSORTED PETITS FOURS

FERRARI-CARANO *Chardonnay 1985*
TUDAL *Cabernet Sauvignon 1983*
IRON HORSE *Brut Rosé 1984*

*President and Mrs. Reagan descend the Grand Staircase with Canadian Prime Minister
Brian Mulroney and Mila Mulroney at the opening of the State Dinner.*

OUR NEIGHBOR TO THE NORTH, Prime Minister Brian Mulroney of Canada, dined at the White House on several occasions in the 1980s. Each time a visit was scheduled, I tried to use Canadian colors and symbols while creating a new dessert. For a dinner on April 27, 1988, I made this pineapple Champagne *sorbet*, served in a *meringue* shell and garnished with maple leaf–shaped cookies and deep red long-stemmed strawberries. I placed a red and white sugar ribbon, to match the colors of the Canadian flag, on top of the dessert. It was served on the Reagan china, which is, not coincidentally, red and white.

At a second dinner, in May 1989, I molded raspberry and *nougat glacé* in bundt pans and garnished each mold with pulled-sugar tulips to celebrate spring. I filled the centers of the molds with assorted red berries in a Grand Marnier sauce and garnished the desserts with maple leaf cookies.

During that visit, we also held an intimate luncheon for the prime minister in the Family Dining Room. I couldn't very well bake those same maple leaf cookies, so I molded some lime and coconut *sorbets* into maple leaves, filled each one with berries, and placed them on top of some caramel sauce. Each one got a decoration of white pulled-sugar tulips, sugar leaves, and a butterfly resting on a leaf.

Pineapple Champagne Sorbet
with Long-Stemmed Strawberries

Dinner, April 27, 1988

SMOKED SALMON AND SHRIMP MOUSSE
DILLED CUCUMBER SAUCE
PETITS CORN STICKS

ROAST LOIN OF VEAL
TARRAGON SAUCE
PURÉE OF SWEET RED PEPPERS
SPRING ASPARAGUS

WATERCRESS AND RADICCHIO SALAD
SAINT PAULIN CHEESE

PINEAPPLE CHAMPAGNE SORBET
PETITS FOURS SEC

SILVERADO *Chardonnay 1986*
WILLIAMS SELYEM *Pinot Noir 1985*
S. ANDERSON *Blanc de Noirs 1983*

45

The bold and spicy flavor of Turkish coffee, traditionally brewed in a long-handled metal pot called an ibrik, is the star of the dessert at the luncheon honoring Turgut Özal, the president of Turkey.

WHEN POSSIBLE, I LET THE GUEST or occasion inspire the flavors of a dessert. The inspiration for the dessert for the luncheon honoring Turgut Özal, president of the Republic of Turkey, came easily: I started with the idea of the very, very strong coffee, often served with spices, that is so beloved in Turkey. The *charlotte* was made with a rich coffee-flavored *mousse* spiced with a cinnamon and cardamom infusion. The decoration was simple but elegant: I covered the top of the *charlotte* with a special coffee glaze to give it a beautiful shine. Then I dipped *meringues* in chocolate and stood them up around the cake. A beautiful pulled-sugar ribbon and bow tied everything up nicely.

Spiced Coffee Charlotte with Chocolate Sauce

Luncheon, September 25, 1990

SMOKED SHRIMP COCKTAIL
HERBED GALETTES

RANCH HOUSE MIXED GRILL
BROILED TOMATO & LEAF SPINACH
GAUFRETTE POTATOES

TOSSED GREEN SALAD

SPICED COFFEE CHARLOTTE
CHOCOLATE SAUCE

SHAFER *Chardonnay 1988*

A table in the State Dining room is set with flowers and candles in preparation for the State Dinner for Queen Margrethe.

FEBRUARY 20, 1991—I still have nightmares about this night, the night I thought would surely be my last at the White House. President George H. W. Bush and First Lady Barbara Bush were entertaining Queen Margrethe II and Prince Henrik of Denmark in the State Dining Room. Since it was the middle of winter, I thought it would be nice to have a hot *soufflé* of *meringue* mixed with fresh raspberry *purée* for the 140 or so guests who would be attending. Mrs. Bush and her social secretary, Laurie Firestone, enthusiastically agreed.

The timing was going to be a challenge. I planned to produce twenty-two large *soufflés* (although there would only be fourteen tables of ten, I had a feeling that most tables would ask for seconds). A three-course dinner usually took about 1 hour to serve. The *soufflés* took 1 hour and 20 minutes to bake. So I knew I'd have to have them in the oven before the guests had even entered the dining room. You must understand one thing about serving a State Dinner: waiting for food is not an option. It must be ready when the *maître d'* says, "Pick up!"—and not a moment later.

I wasn't too worried. I had tested and retested my recipe, watching the clock every time. All of my ingredients were premeasured, and at just the right moment I began to whip my egg whites, eighty at a time. But something was wrong: they weren't coming up the way they should have. This had never happened to me. I began to sweat. I cleaned the bowl and beaters and started again. Again, my whites refused to cooperate.

While I was cleaning the bowl for the third time, I overheard the executive chef and the *sous* chef discussing the mayonnaise they had made earlier in the day. They must have prepared it in this machine! If even a trace of oil remained behind in the openings where the beaters were inserted into the machine, it would drip back into the bowl when they were reinserted after cleaning. Now I cleaned these spots, too, and was finally on my way. But I had lost so much time that I was worried I wouldn't make it. As I played catch-up, many thoughts, none of them pleasant, crossed my mind. I'd have to tell the first lady that we wouldn't have dessert that night. I'd soon be standing on the unemployment line. I'd be flipping burgers in a downtown fast-food restaurant.

At the same time, I was thinking of ways to rescue the *soufflés*. I turned the oven up higher and placed the *soufflés* on trays that I put right on top of the gas burner to preheat them before baking. I was able to make up the time. They started coming out of the oven, looking great. And just as the first ones were ready, I heard the first of twenty-two calls of, "Pick up!" "Let's rock and roll!" I was able to reply, as I put the first *soufflé* onto the first butler's beautiful silver tray, lined with pretty napkins, so he could take it upstairs to the dining room. After that, everything proceeded according to plan, including the requests for seconds, which I was able to supply with no problem. What a night of terror and triumph combined! I will never forget it as long as I live!

Hot Raspberry Soufflé

Dinner, February 20, 1991

LOBSTER MÉDAILLONS &
  CUCUMBER MOUSSE
CAVIAR SAUCE
GRUYÈRE BOW TIES

CROWN ROAST OF LAMB
JALAPEÑO MINT SAUCE
CROQUETTE POTATOES
CARROT TIMBALE WITH SNOW PEAS

ENDIVE, WATERCRESS & MUSHROOM
  SALAD
NATIVE CHÈVRE CHEESE, MELBA TOAST

HOT RASPBERRY SOUFFLÉ
CUSTARD SAUCE
PETITS FOURS

SANFORD *Chardonnay Barrel Select 1988*
ROBERT MONDAVI *Pinot Noir Reserve 1988*
VICHON *Sémillion Botrytis 1987*

*President and Mrs. Bush welcome Queen Elizabeth II and Prince Philip of the United Kingdom
to the White House prior to the State Dinner.*

ALL VISITING HEADS OF STATE and dignitaries are welcomed with fanfare at the White House, but few dignitaries generate the level of excitement as Queen Elizabeth II and Prince Philip.

When the dinner was planned, Laurie Firestone, Mrs. Bush's social secretary, gave us the order to "Go all out." The Usher's Office, which coordinates the various units in the White House residence such as the kitchen, the Flower Shop, the painters, and housekeeping, was also putting the pressure on. Expectations were high. The dessert had to be pure magic. There was also the pressure I put on myself. I had served the British royal family many times, as a pastry chef at London's famed Savoy Hotel, as the pastry chef to the governor of Bermuda (when a young Prince Charles came to the island for the opening of the new Bermuda Parliament building, I created a model out of sugar for the occasion), and quite a few times at the White House. Each time, I was well aware of how well traveled and well fed these very special diners were. Pastry chefs all over the world were constantly trying to top one another when serving the queen of England, and I am as competitive as the next one!

I decided to fashion something out of a fairy tale, a chocolate carriage sitting on a *marzipan* "cobblestone" street. The carriage would be filled with pistachio *marquise*, a dense *mousse*, layered with crunchy *meringue* and *nougat*. I'd cover the *marquise* with raspberries so it would look like the carriage was filled with them.

It's one thing to imagine a dessert, and another thing to actually make it. This one was a feat of engineering as well as of pastry. I used a technique similar to the one I used to make the Chinese junk (for the State Dinner for China in 1984), carving a carriage from wood. I used that carving to make a silicone mold, which in turn I used to mold the chocolate shell of each carriage, for a total of fifteen. To make the wheels, I pressed wooden models of wheels into a tray of cocoa powder and then poured chocolate into the impressions. Once the wheels had hardened, I fixed a chocolate band around each one.

The coach shows how it was designed to remain standing even if the diners snapped off and ate all four wheels. This is the kind of thing I always tried to anticipate, especially with President George H. W. Bush. I had noticed years earlier, when he was vice president under President Reagan, that he liked to taste every single element of the dessert. I couldn't very well send out a dessert that would collapse into pieces as he nibbled here and there!

Pistachio Marquise with Fresh Raspberries

Dinner, May 14, 1991

MEDALLIONS OF MAINE LOBSTER AND
  CUCUMBER MOUSSE
AURORA SAUCE
GALETTES FINES HERBES

CROWN ROAST OF LAMB
DAUPHINE POTATOES
BOUQUETTES OF VEGETABLES

WATERCRESS AND
  BELGIAN ENDIVE SALAD

ST. ANDRE AND CHEVRE CHEESE

PISTACHIO MARQUISE WITH
  FRESH RASPBERRIES

SWANSON *Reserve Chardonnay 1988*
SHAFER HILLSIDE
  Select Cabernet Sauvignon 1986
JORDAN, *J 1987*

Bermuda's famous beaches inspired the design for a dessert featuring sea creatures.

WHEN I HEARD THE NEWS that the Bermuda Premier John Swan and Lady Jacqueline Swan were going to have dinner with President and Mrs. George H. W. Bush, I was very excited. I knew John Swan personally from his days as a prominent real estate entrepreneur and respected citizen when I was pastry chef at the Princess Hotel. In fact, he had been the landlord of my first apartment in Hamilton, and every month I had paid my rent directly to him!

I was determined to let him know at the dinner that there was someone in the White House who was representing Bermuda very well. So I got on the telephone to a friend of mine, Axel Heinicke, the purchasing manager at the Southampton Princess, and I told him that I needed two bottles of Bermuda Gold (a rum-based liqueur flavored with loquat, an exotic fruit transplanted from Asia to Bermuda in the nineteenth century) that I knew well from my time on the island. I did not care how he did it and what it cost, but it had to be at the White House in 24 hours. Axel came through like a champion, and the Bermuda Gold—more than I required for the dinner, happily—arrived in plenty of time.

With this key ingredient secured, I decided to make a dessert with a maritime look—a white chocolate shell filled with fishes, seashells, lobsters, and sea urchins, all made of different flavored *sorbets* and ice creams, each one with a different filling in its center. The shell would be decorated with chocolate seaweed and different colored chocolate fish swimming around the shell in every direction. Fresh fruit would garnish the platter, and the exquisite Bermuda Gold *sabayon* sauce would be served on the side. Delicate cookies passed with coffee topped off the evening.

A few years later, when my book *Dessert University* came out, I was invited by the Princess Hotel management to a few special dinners and book signings to mark the occasion. After one of those dinners, during which I had described John Swan's dessert, a beautiful and gracious young woman approached me to introduce herself. She was John Swan's daughter, and she wanted to thank me for being a part of that special White House evening and for making her father so happy. She spent the rest of the evening with me, my wife, and some of our old Princess Hotel friends, reminiscing and celebrating that lovely island.

Chocolate Seashells
with Assorted Sorbets & Bermuda Gold Sabayon

Dinner, May 19, 1992

CONSOMMÉ OF PHEASANT
MUSHROOM RISSOLES

CHÂTEAUBRIAND, BEARNAISE SAUCE
GAUFRETTE POTATOES
GREEN ASPARAGUS
TOMATO-CORN FERMIÉRE

SPRING SALAD
BLUE AND TRAPPIST CHEESE

CHOCOLATE SEA SHELL WITH
 ASSORTED SORBET
BERMUDA GOLD SABAYON
COOKIES

SAINTSBURY *Chardonnay 1990*
SHAFER *Cabernet Sauvignon 1986*
SCHARFFENBERGER *Blanc de Blancs*

Russian President Boris Yeltsin and his wife Naina Yeltsin descend the Grand Staircase with President and Mrs. George H. W. Bush for the formal ceremonies before the State Dinner.

*P*RESIDENT BORIS YELTSIN was one of the most colorful heads of state I observed during my years at the White House. Judging from the smiling and laughing photos I've seen of President Yeltsin with our U.S. presidents, he got along quite well with his hosts.

When Mr. Yeltsin visited as the guest of President and Mrs. George H. W. Bush, the kitchen had California sturgeon flown in for the first time. President Bush was probably the most adventurous eater I worked for and always wanted to try new foods. The dessert was a caramel and roasted dried pear *mousse* layered with lady finger biscuits that had been soaked with a light pear brandy syrup. A light orange sauce was poured around the *mousse*, and then roasted dried pears filled with orange segments and glazed candied orange peel were placed on top of the sauce. The shiny glaze on top gave this dessert its nice finish, along with some very fine piping and pistachio pieces. I couldn't resist adorning the dessert with a bouquet of pulled-sugar black-eyed Susans, a flower often grown in Russia.

Caramel and Roasted Dried Pear Mousse
with Orange Grand Marnier Sauce

Dinner, June 16, 1992

CALIFORNIA BELUSA STURGEON
SAUCE DIPLOMAT
SESAME GALETTES

ROAST LOIN OF VEAL AMBASSADEUR
WILD MUSHROOM SAUCE
DUCHESSE POTATOES
GREEN ASPARAGUS & BABY CARROTS

SUMMER SALAD
HERBED CAPRI CHEESE

CARAMEL MOUSSE WITH ROASTED
 DRIED PEARS
ORANGE SAUCE
COOKIES

CAKEBREAD *Sauvignon Blanc 1990*
SANFORD *Barrel Select Pinot Noir 1989*
GABRIELE Y CAROLINE
 Late Harvest Riesling 1982

Petits fours disguised as sushi rolls are a nod to Japan's famous delicacies.

T HAD BEEN SIX-TEEN YEARS since the last State Dinner for the Emperor of Japan, Hirohito. So it was a very big deal when this one, to honor his son, the Emperor Akihito, was announced. It would be a white-tie affair, the most elaborate and fancy of all White House dinners—held in the Rose Garden. First Lady Hillary Clinton and her social secretary, Ann Stock, thought through every detail and held a rehearsal before the actual event to make sure that everything went smoothly. The food was tasted, the timing of each course was checked and adjusted according to a minute-by-minute schedule, the table settings were tweaked. Nothing was left to chance.

For my part, I wanted to make a dessert like nothing I had ever made before. I thought about the friendship between Japan and the United States that is symbolized by the famous cherry trees in the Tidal Basin of Washington. These trees were a gift from Japan to the United States in 1912. The first one was planted by First Lady Helen Herron Taft and is still alive and thriving, alongside more than three thousand others. With this idea in mind, I asked Mrs. Clinton for permission to make large platters instead of individual plated desserts. In my experience, having the butlers parade into the dining room with platters has a much bigger impact than serving single portions.

When Mrs. Clinton agreed, I got to work. I blew some big red sugar balls, each one the size of a football. After I cut them in half using a special Dremel saw, I fixed the opened balls, which resembled open cherries,

onto white chocolate bases. Each cherry was decorated with some sugar cherry blossoms on a stem. White almond ice cream balls filled with red cherry *sorbet* were placed inside each opened cherry. When the guests dug into the ice cream, they'd find the *sorbet* as a surprise. I hoped they'd notice that the red center and its white background resembled the Japanese flag. The base of the big cherry was garnished with hand-pitted fresh cherries flown in from California specially for this occasion. Poached kumquat tartlets were served on the side, with a wild strawberry sauce. The *petits fours* were all shaped like sushi—sea urchin, lotus root, shrimp. Colored chocolate bands resembling nori wrapped cookies that looked like sliced sushi rolls. Even the bamboo handle of the sushi basket was made of sugar.

Although putting together all of the components of the dessert demanded the full attention of the pastry and service staff, it was a lot of fun. The butlers had never seen anything like it, and were delighted to carry the platters and *petits fours* out to prominent guests, including Oprah Winfrey, Jane Fonda, and Barbra Streisand, as well as many prominent politicians and business figures. The setup was grand, with round tables arranged around a head table, all the trees in the Rose Garden covered with tiny little lights. The tent looked fantastic—the best I'd ever seen it. Later I found out that Empress Michiko wanted to congratulate me in person on the dessert, but her schedule and protocol hadn't allowed. Nevertheless, I felt rewarded to have been a part of this exciting dinner.

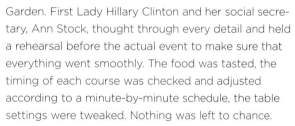

Cherry Sherbet
with Almond Milk Ice Cream, California Cherries and
Wild Strawberry Sauce, "Sushi" Baskets

Dinner, June 13, 1994

SEARED BREAST OF QUAIL
WHITE CORN CUSTARD & GRILLED
  VEGETABLES, TOMATO-CUMIN SAUCE

GRILLED ARCTIC CHAR AND LOBSTER
  SAUSAGE
WILD MUSHROOM RISOTTO, BRAISED
  FENNEL, VEGETABLE RAGOUT,
  ROASTED GARLIC AND LIME SAUCE

FIELD GREENS WITH GOAT CHEESE &
  BASIL IN PHYLLO, PORT WINE DRESSING

CHERRY SHERBET WITH ALMOND
  ICE CREAM
CALIFORNIA "BERKLEY" CHERRIES
WILD STRAWBERRY SAUCE
"SUSHI" BASKET

KISTLER *"Sand Hill" Chardonnay 1992*
DOMAINE DROUHIN *"Oregon" Pinot Noir 1992*
ROEDERER ESTATE *"Extra Dry"*
  White House Cuvée

Tony Bennett, seen here with President Clinton, performed for guests in the East Room of the White House following the State Dinner for German Chancellor Helmut Kohl.

*I*T WAS STILL WINTER in Washington, and the State Dining Room was glowing and glittering, the tables set with the Reagan china service. For this time of year, I chose deep and comforting flavors of hazelnuts, coffee, and rum. I love using beautifully crafted Old World ice cream molds and thought that Chancellor Helmut Kohl would appreciate a molded ice cream dessert, since there is a strong tradition in Germany of hand-crafting beautiful molds. (The one I used was made by hand in Greece with copper on the outside and food-safe stainless steel on the inside.) So I made a hazelnut ice cream mold filled with coffee rum *mousse* and crunchy *meringue*. I decorated each one with *nougat* triangles and red polka-dotted *meringue* mushrooms. If you look closely at the green leaves, you can see whole blanched hazelnuts nestled among them. The *petit four* tray I am displaying holds rich goodies just right for the season: Parisian macaroons, chocolate almond drops, and butter cookies dipped in chocolate.

Most of my work, over the years, was performed in the White House pastry kitchen. But occasionally I traveled with the president to different locations where he entertained various heads of state during important meetings. The 1997 G7 summit in Denver was one memorable trip, and there I once again had the opportunity to prepare desserts that appealed to Chancellor Kohl's tastes.

Coffee and Hazelnut Ice Cream Mold

Dinner, February 9, 1995

HERB ROASTED PHEASANT BREAST
WILD MUSHROOM RISOTTO
TOMATO BASIL COULIS

PAN SEARED SALMON LOIN WITH
  KEY LIME AND GINGER
ORIENTAL VEGETABLE CONFETTI
RICE NOODLE CRISPS

MARINATED GOAT CHEESE AND
  VEGETABLE TERRINE WITH
  YOUNG GREENS, BALSAMIC DRESSING

COFFEE AND ROASTED HAZELNUT
  ICE MOLD
CINNAMON SABAYON AND LIGHT
  CHOCOLATE SAUCE
BASKET OF MACAROONS

SOLITUDE *Chardonnay 1993*
LA BOHEME *Pinot Noir 1992*
SCHRAMSBERG *Crémant Demi-sec 1991*

*Pakistani Prime Minister Benazir Bhutto visits Chef Mesnier's pastry kitchen
after a White House luncheon in her honor.*

FIRST LADY HILLARY CLINTON was a great admirer of Benazir Bhutto, the prime minister of Pakistan, so I wanted to do my best to make something beautiful and special to please them both at the end of this very special luncheon. A pecan ice cream dome was just the thing. The background was made of honey *nougat* and fresh pistachios decorated with royal icing and pulled-sugar wild roses and leaves. I surrounded the ice cream dome with some of the *nougat* pieces, to make them more accessible to guests who wanted a taste. The bananas are the baby variety, which I picked up at the market myself. What luck! They aren't always available, and they have a more concentrated flavor than the larger fruit. The crispy, buttery *phyllo* dough was a wonderful contrast with the creamy, sweet bananas inside.

As the luncheon came to an end, Mrs. Clinton and Mrs. Bhutto talked about the many impressive works of art in the White House. Mrs. Bhutto then complimented the dessert for its beauty, and said she'd like to take the pastry chef back to Pakistan! Mrs. Clinton replied with laughter that she could have any other White House treasure, but not me! And then, much to my surprise, they took the small elevator from the dining room to my kitchen for an unscheduled visit, accompanied by Mrs. Bhutto's entourage and mother. I was thrilled and honored to show everyone my sugar work, safely kept behind glass in special cabinets. After photographs were taken, we said good-bye. It was a humbling and special day.

I was so saddened to read of Mrs. Bhutto's brutal assassination in her own country. It was a shocking reminder of how vulnerable heads of state are, even as they sit in positions of the highest power. She will be in my heart forever. What a great lady.

Baked Bananas in Phyllo Dough
with Pecan Ice Cream and Caramel Sauce

Luncheon, April 11, 1995

BRAISED CHICKEN & LENTILS
LEEKS & SUMMER SQUASH

GRILLED LOIN OF LAMB WITH SAFFRON
ROASTED ONION, ALMOND &
   CUMIN SAUCE
VEGETABLE BIRYANI & POPPADOMS

YOUNG GREENS WITH PAPAYA &
   PINEAPPLE
POMEGRANATE DRESSING

PECAN ICE CREAM
CARAMEL SAUCE

JOSEPH PHELPS *Viognier 1993*

The dessert for Egyptian President Hosni Mubarak echoes the shape of the famous pyramids of Giza.

OVER THE YEARS I made so many desserts for President Hosni Mubarak that it was difficult to select a particular favorite. These two are definitely in the running. Each one borrows its shape from the Great Pyramid and uses flavors popular in Middle Eastern cooking. But beyond this they are very different from each other. The first one is my vision of ancient Egypt. The second is a nod to modern Egyptian architecture.

The "Citrus Pyramid" was molded from lemon *sorbet* filled with date *mousse* and pistachio *nougat*. A date *sabayon* was served on the side. I can't think of a better combination of flavors! Surrounding the pyramid is an abundance of fresh lychees, raspberries, and blackberries. It is a refined pyramid, decorated with delicately piped chocolate flowers and leaves.

In contrast, the "Raspberry and Cantaloupe Sorbet Pyramid" was completely over the top! The *sorbet* pyramid was sitting atop another upside down pyramid made of almond *nougat*. A lavender honey *sabayon* was served on the side. A riot of fresh fruit surrounded what appeared to be a precariously balanced dessert. I made date shortbread for the *petit four* trays. The pyramid didn't let me down. Compliments poured in from the dining room on this fun and flavorful version.

Citrus Pyramid
with Date Mousse and Pistachio Nougat

Luncheon, April 5, 1995

MULTI-COLORED PASTA WITH
 GRILLED SALMON
ONION TOMATILLO SAUCE

SEARED LOIN OF VENISON IN
 PHYLLO CRUST
WILD MUSHROOMS AND SECKEL PEAR

SPRING GREENS WITH SWEET
 POTATO CRISPS
BALSAMIC DRESSING

CITRUS PYRAMID
DATE SABAYON
MINIATURE BAKLAVA

FLORA SPRINGS *Chardonnay 1991*

63

President Clinton and French President Jacques Chirac descend from the reviewing stand after delivering remarks on the South Lawn during the arrival ceremony.

*a*LTHOUGH I BECAME A U.S. CITIZEN when I began working at the White House, I was born in France and have a strong bond with the country where my brothers and sisters still live. During my years at the White House, I had many chances to make dessert for French leaders. These occasions were always memorable and a little emotional for me. I remember a visit by President François Mitterrand during the Reagan administration. In spite of my hopes to meet him, I never managed to gain an audience.

But there were many French VIPs whom I did meet. Mrs. Clinton, especially, would go out of her way to call me from the kitchen to introduce me to French visitors. She kindly invited me to the Clintons' private quarters for a meeting with Prime Minister Lionel Jospin. When President Jacques Chirac visited for this particular dinner, she asked me to come to the newly decorated Blue Room so we could be introduced. He was extremely cordial and friendly.

I had been busy preparing that evening's *croquembouche*, a traditional French dessert with an American twist. Instead of making the pyramid of caramel-coated cream puffs familiar to every French citizen, I planned to alternate caramel puffs with rows of apple and cherry *sorbet* shaped like lady apples. The puffs and *sorbet* balls were all to be attached to a cone of green apple *sorbet*. Because the *sorbet* had to be ice cold and the cream puffs had to be at room temperature, the dessert had to be assembled just before serving. And as you can see, the assembly is quite complicated! I knew this going in, but I was not willing to compromise on the idea, so my assistants and I very quickly, and under extreme pressure, put all sixteen *croquembouches* together in minutes. We set cream-puff swans to swim in a pool of raspberry sauce around the bases and placed spun-sugar decorations that looked like the *panache* of the helmets of the Republican guards at the Élysée Palace on the top of each cone. We were just finishing when the White House butlers strode into the kitchen calling "Pick up!"—meaning the diners were ready for dessert. The next day I bumped into President Clinton, who told me that the *croquembouches* were admired by the French and Americans alike, making them well worth the effort!

Croquembouche of Apple and Cherry Sorbet

Dinner, February 1, 1996

LEMON THYME LOBSTER WITH ROASTED
  EGGPLANT SOUP

RACK OF LAMB WITH WINTER FRUIT
  AND PECANS, SWEET POTATO PURÉE,
  ROOT VEGETABLES, TARRAGON
  HUCKLEBERRY SAUCE

LAYERED ARTICHOKE, LEEK AND
  HERBED CHEESE WITH GREENS AND
  ENDIVE, BALSAMIC DRESSING

APPLE AND CHERRY SHERBET PYRAMID
APPLE BRANDY SAUCE
PEANUT BUTTER TRUFFLES
WHITE ALMOND BARK CHOCOLATE
  FUDGE

BERINGÉR *Viognier 1994*
ZACA MESA *Syrah 1993*
ROEDERER ESTATES *L'Ermitage 1990*

Italian President Oscar Luigi Scalfaro and his daughter Marianna Scalfaro are greeted by President and Mrs. Clinton upon their arrival at the White House for the State Dinner in his honor.

OVER THE YEARS, my inspiration for State Dinner desserts came from various sources. I never looked to politics for inspiration, but rather looked for something that would help create warm feelings between the first family and the visiting head of state by honoring his or her country. Sometimes it was something I remembered seeing during a visit to a particular country—a building, a painting, a natural wonder—that inspired a dessert. Sometimes it was a particular food or flavor associated with a place.

This particular dessert doesn't scream "Italy" at first glance, but it was designed with the delicious strawberry crop that Italians enjoy very early in the calendar year in mind. Lemons, almonds, chestnuts, and pistachios also reflect the bounty of Italy. To pay tribute to these big flavors, I created a giant, free-form strawberry made of strawberry *sorbet*, garnished with pulled-sugar strawberry blossoms and leaves. Pieces of pistachio were pushed into the strawberry to look like strawberry seeds. I filled the strawberry with an Amaretto *parfait* and Italian white almond *nougat mousse* with pieces of chestnut and crushed macaroons. Fresh seasonal fruit adorned each platter (I always tried to provide a low-calorie dessert option for people who were watching their diets), and lemon *crème brûlée* was offered on the side (for people who were willing to throw caution to the wind!).

I found this dessert to be spectacular! The *petit four* tray was also bursting with Italian flavors and equally spectacular in presentation, garnished as it was with sugar swans swimming on a lagoon edged with sugar rock formations. Three *petits fours* were offered: Italian *nougat* dipped in chocolate, miniature almond *soufflés*, and tiny gondolas made of chestnut cream and glazed with vanilla on one side and chocolate on the other.

Strawberry Surprise

Dinner, April 2, 1996

CHILLED SPRING PEA AND
   ZUCCHINI SOUP
HERB MARINATED YOUNG VEGETABLES
LAMB LOIN WITH BASIL POLENTA,
   PORTABELLO MUSHROOM, ROASTED
   PEPPERS AND FAVA BEAN RAGOUT
BAROLO SAUCE

YOUNG LETTUCES AND SPROUTS
LAYERED ASIAGO AND GOAT'S CHEESE
RHUBARB DRESSING

STRAWBERRY SURPRISE
LEMON BURNED CREAM
ALMOND PISTACHIO NOUGAT
CHESTNUT GONDOLA

GALLO *"Estate" Chardonnay 1993*
MONDAVI *"Reserve" Cabernet 1990*
SILVAN RIDGE *"Early Muscat" 1994*

Elements of Greek architecture are reflected in the dessert for President Constantinos Stephanopoulos.

T O FRAME THIS DESSERT, I wanted to use some of the bold and strong architectural elements of ancient Greece. So I molded columns of different sizes in white chocolate. Draped between the columns are flags, made of *décor* chocolate, with the colors of Greece and the United States. The dessert itself is a marbleized dome (the technique is one of my professional secrets!) of lemon *sorbet* filled with honey *parfait* that had been mixed with some crushed almond *meringue* and *nougat*, for texture. Fresh strawberries and raspberries ringed the dome. Just before serving, we poured dark chocolate onto each platter and piped the Greek key motif around the edge in white chocolate. That was a nice Greek touch, and looked great with the columns.

A black raspberry sauce and fresh fruit were served as an accompaniment. The *petit four* tray featured Greek-style cookies including mini-*baklavas*, pine nut macaroons, and *kourabiedes*. I was proud that the ending to this State Dinner was such a successful tribute to Greek style and flavor.

Dome of Lemon Sorbet and Honey Parfait

Dinner, May 9, 1996

ROASTED TOMATO WITH SMOKED BASIL
SHRIMP, FAVA BEANS AND EGGPLANT
SALAD, POTATO GARLIC SAUCE

GRILLED LAMB TENDERLOIN WITH
SPINACH ORZO, SPICY OLIVE SLIVERS
AND CRISPY BEETS, YELLOW PEPPER
REDUCTION

MARINATED YOUNG GREENS, WARM
KEFALOTIRI CHEESE AND BAKED FIGS
ORANGE SAFFRON DRESSING

LEMON HONEY MARBLEIZED DOME
BLACK RASPBERRY SAUCE WITH
  SEASONAL FRUIT
BAKLAVA, PINE NUT MACAROONS AND
  KOURABIEDES

LOLONIS *Chardonnay "Reserve" 1994*
TOPOLOS *Zinfandel "Piner Heights" 1994*
PINDAR *Brut "Long Island" 1989*

British Prime Minister Tony Blair and President Clinton greet actor Harrison Ford, a dinner guest,
in the receiving line for the State Dinner at the White House.

BRITISH PRIME MINISTER TONY BLAIR and President Clinton had a close relationship, so when a State Dinner was scheduled, it went without saying that the event would be grand, exciting, and special. After consulting with the Social Secretary's Office, I determined that the dessert for this dinner would be an elaborate tribute to England. To that end, I began to create dark chocolate baskets, each one to be decorated with baroque colored chocolate ornaments and then to be filled with a mixture of lemon curd and Devonshire cream, a slightly tart, thick clotted cream that doesn't have to be whipped and is beloved by the English. Strawberries poached just enough to soften them while allowing them to keep their shape and fresh flavor would be placed on top of the cream. The green leaves that you see between the berries were piped with buttercream. Making and attaching the chocolate ornaments was a chore. I made each ornament on a flat surface and then very slowly and carefully warmed it enough so I could bend it to fit around the basket. In addition, I embellished each basket with a white pulled-sugar rose. The dinner was large, so I needed twenty-five ornamented baskets.

But the baskets were nothing compared with the drama of the *petit four* trays. To accompany this undoubtedly English dessert, I had planned to decorate each tray with a chocolate Big Ben as a decoration.

Two weeks before the dinner, I spoke to Derek Rooke, the pastry chef at my old London stomping ground, the Savoy Hotel, to see if he could send me a model of Big Ben that I could use to create a silicone mold for producing my chocolate decorations. He promised to post it right away, but two days before the dinner it still hadn't arrived. During several desperate phone calls Derek assured me that it was on the way, but this didn't alleviate my panic when I ran into the first lady and confided to her my despair over the missing model. At 10:00 a.m. on the day of the dinner, my Big Ben finally materialized, too late for me to make the chocolate mold as I'd planned. But I was determined to use it for the evening's dessert. So I quickly made a giant batch of butter cookie dough, rolled it out, laid sheets of plastic wrap on top of it, and pressed the Big Ben into the dough so it left three-sided impressions. Then I froze the dough, filled the impressions with melted chocolate, and froze the filled dough until the chocolate was solid. To hide the plain back of each Big Ben I cut out some flat pieces of white chocolate and glued them on, painting some white clouds against the blue sky. I finished the twenty-fifth Big Ben at 6:45 p.m., just as the dinner was getting under way, in time to place the brandy snaps, shortbread, honey nougat, and chocolate fudge around each one (see page 6). What a thrilling day. It had taken every ounce of my energy and experience to pull it off.

Strawberries and Cream
with Devonshire Sauce

Dinner, February 5, 1998

HONEY MANGO GLAZED CHICKEN
SPICY VEGETABLE "NOODLES"
HERB TUILE

GRILLED SALMON FILLET "MIGNON"
SEARED PORTOBELLO MUSHROOM,
  TOMATO SHALLOT FONDUE
BABY VEGETABLES AND BALSAMIC
  REDUCTION

MARINATED FRESH MOZZARELLA,
ROASTED ARTICHOKES AND BASIL
TOMATOES

SALAD OF MACHE AND ARUGULA,
  LEMON OREGANO DRESSING

"STRAWBERRIES AND CREAM"
DEVONSHIRE SAUCE
BRANDY SNAPS, SHORT BREAD, HONEY
  NOUGAT, CHOCOLATE FUDGE

NEWTON *Chardonnay "Unfiltered" 1995*
SWANSON *Sangiovese 1995*
MUMM *Napa Valley "DVX" 1993*

President Clinton reviews U.S. troops with Italian Prime Minister Romano Prodi during arrival ceremonies at the White House. It was Professor Prodi's first State Visit to the United States.

WHEN I VISITED the Italian Embassy in preparation for this dinner, I discovered that Professor Romano Prodi was originally from Bologna, where there are two well-known medieval towers. A little more research revealed to me that peaches and chestnuts are popular in that region of Italy. From my own travels, I knew that Italians are very fond of rich cakes soaked in liqueur and filled with custard cream.

That's all the information I needed to create this dessert, a *brioche* cake soaked in Amaretto syrup, filled with vanilla custard and fresh peach slices, and covered in honey *meringue*. Chestnut *parfait*, chocolate and caramel sauces, and a *petit four* platter of traditional Italian treats—*sfogliatelle*, *zeppole*, *amaretti*—accompanied the cake. The *pièce de résistance* was a replica of one of the Bolognese towers, made of chestnut ice cream and decorated with *nougat* pieces. The blue gazebo on top was made of colored sugar. I designed the tower so that even after the ice cream was eaten, the gazebo remained in place. Every platter came back to the kitchen with the gazebo still standing.

I was told by the butlers that Professor Prodi was very touched to see the tower from his birthplace re-created for his pleasure at the White House. From their report, he had a tear in his eye when he took his first bite.

A Tribute to Bologna

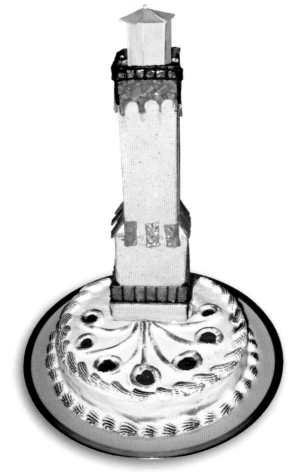

Dinner, May 6, 1998

TART OF SPRING VEGETABLE
ARTICHOKE AND FIDDLEHEAD FERNS
MEYER LEMON & WILD LEEK DRESSING

GRILLED ALASKAN HALIBUT
COULIS OF FRESH GREEN PEAS
GREMOLATA RISOTTO
OREGON MORELS, ASPARAGUS
  & FAVA BEANS

SALAD OF PURSLANE AND YOUNG
  GREENS

CHARRED VIDALIA ONIONS, MANGO &
  AVOCADO, CURRIED BASIL DRESSING

A TRIBUTE TO BOLOGNA
PEACH CAKE WITH CHESTNUT PARFAIT
CHOCOLATE CARAMEL SAUCE
SFOGLIATELLE, ZEPPOLE AND AMARETTI

PONZI *Arneis 1996*
HORTON *Nebbiolo 1995*
PECOTA *Moscato d'Andrea 1997*
ROEDERER *"White House Cuvee" 1991*

*Tango dancers glide gracefully across a chocolate floor in this dessert
for the dinner in honor of the Argentine president.*

ARLY IN MY TENURE at the White House, I realized that while it was a good idea to make desserts that very clearly honored the foods and flavors of a particular country, I had to design dishes that were my own rather than trying to reproduce a beloved standard from a particular place. I could never make a *tiramisu* to match the memories of the one that the Italian prime minister ate as a child, or present a *baklava* that the Greek president wouldn't inevitably compare to the others he had eaten. So that's not the direction I was going to take. Instead, I trod carefully, aiming to make an impression by creating a chocolate or sugar sculpture that captured the spirit of a visiting head of state's home while steering clear of any images that might offend or cause controversy. It wasn't always easy.

One great place to start learning about a country is its embassy, so very often when a State Dinner was put on the schedule I'd immediately make a visit, hoping that someone there would give me some good ideas. So as soon as I heard that the president of

Argentina would be honored, I called the Argentine Embassy to make an appointment, and on a sunny autumn afternoon I found myself chatting about typical Argentine food with the ambassador himself. He could not have been more welcoming and enthusiastic as he described Argentine beef, going so far as to invite me to his weekly barbecue. My mouth was watering. When we got around to discussing dessert, we did not get beyond the idea of a cow molded in chocolate.

I wanted something spectacular, so it was back to the drawing board. It took quite a few days of thumbing through books and pamphlets until I spotted a small picture of some graceful tango dancers. That was it. I made a small prototype that I brought to the first lady for approval, explaining that the dessert itself, a frozen *dulce de leche* served with roasted pineapple, coconut snowballs, and caramel walnuts, would focus on Argentine flavors. She was delighted with the idea, since it complemented the evening's entertainment: the actor Robert Duvall and his beautiful Argentine wife, Luciana Pedraza, performing a tango!

Frozen Dulce de Leche

Dinner, January 11, 1999

LEMON HERB ROASTED CHICKEN
GRILLED VEGETABLE RISOTTO
TOMATO BASIL BROTH

SEARED STRIPED BASS
CASSOULET OF JONAH CRAB, CORN
   AND FAVA BEANS
SAUTÉED MORELS AND SWEET POTATO

SALAD OF WINTER GREENS, ENDIVE
   AND SPINACH

BLEU CHEESE FRITTER
SHERRY AND PANCETTA DRESSING

FROZEN DULCE DE LECHE
BAKED PINEAPPLE
CARAMEL WALNUTS
COCONUT SNOWBALLS

SANFORD *Chardonnay "Estate" 1996*
BEAUX FRERES *Pinot Noir 1995*
MUMM *Cuvee Napa "DVX" 1993*

A U-shaped table set for the NATO Summit dinner in the East Room is decorated with white hydrangea, white dendrobiums, gardenias, green grapes, white roses, smilax, and maiden hair ferns.

*Y*HIS WAS A HISTORIC TWO-DAY EVENT, with a large dinner on the South Lawn in a pavilion and then a dinner the next day to celebrate the founding of the North Atlantic Treaty Organization. About nine hundred people attended the first event. I had never seen so many leaders under one tent. Individual chocolate and praline cakes were inscribed, "NATO 50th Summit—The White House." They were accompanied by vanilla sauce, fresh strawberries, and orange segments.

The dinner the next day in the East Room was a smaller affair, for about sixty people. The crescent-shaped table was exquisite, set with vermeil serving pieces and decorated with white hydrangeas, white dendrobiums, gardenias, and white roses with green ferns. The dessert, served on platters from the Truman china service, was a showstopper. I placed domes of strawberry *nougat glacé* on blue sugar stands set upon solid dark chocolate bases. I had drilled tiny holes into the chocolate at an angle, for the flags, each representing a country attending the summit. Each flag was hand-painted on sugar or *pastillage*, some more complicated than others. It took several weeks and many staff members to perform that tedious job, but I was so happy with the result. To finish the presentation, we garnished the platters with sliced strawberries and kiwis and passed Champagne *sabayon*, small chocolate globe truffles, and passion fruit *tuiles*. Fabulous!

Strawberry Nougat Glacé
with Champagne Sabayon

Dinner, April 23, 1999

CRISPY SOFT SHELL CRAB WITH
  BLUE CRAB AND LOBSTER CAKES
FENNEL AND CORN SLAW
CUCUMBER MINT COULIS

SPRING LAMB WITH LEMON-LAVENDER
CONFIT OF PORTOBELLO AND
  SWEET PEPPERS
FAVA BEAN PURÉE, MAUI ONION SAUCE

SALAD OF LOLO ROSO, RED MUSTARD

AND UPLAND CRESS, BAKED GOAT
CHEESE, AGED BALSAMIC VINAIGRETTE

"A SALUTE TO NATO"
STRAWBERRY NOUGAT GLACÉ
CHAMPAGNE SABAYON, CHOCOLATE
  GLOBE, PASSION FRUIT TUILES

ANCIEN *Chardonnay 1997*
FLOWERS *Pinot Noir "Camp Meeting Ridge" 1996*
PAUMANOK *Late Harvest Sauvignon Blanc 1997*

President and Mrs. Clinton pose with Japanese Prime Minister Keizō Obuchi and his wife Chizuko on the North Portico of the White House.

HE STATE DINNER honoring the Japanese Prime Minister Keizō Obuchi was an unusually large and elaborate one, served under a pavilion erected on the South Lawn of the White House for the occasion. The pavilion itself was comfortable and even luxurious, with air-conditioning, chandeliers, carpets, and beautifully illuminated trees. I decided on individual plated desserts for the formal occasion, instead of the more casual Russian service that I often employed for State Dinners held indoors. Individual desserts would also allow me to create a miniature Japanese tableau for each diner, which I felt was a perfect way to honor our guests.

On each plate was a small almond and orange *mousse* cake, decorated with a disk of red jelly to look like the Japanese flag, set next to a small river of kiwi sauce, upon which some tiny sugar flowers floated. Sliced blood oranges garnished the cake. A chocolate bridge and *bonsai* tree completed the scene.

Did I mention that we had to produce 650 of these desserts? I started working on the bridges and trees weeks before the event, and baked the cakes several days in advance. It took many hours of preparation on the day of the dinner to ensure that all 650 would be ready in time for service. Shortly before the dinner got started, Prime Minister Obuchi himself peeked into the kitchen and saw some of the hundreds of chocolate bridges and trees. He thanked us graciously for our hard work!

A Bonsai Garden of Sweet Serenity

Dinner, May 3, 1999

GINGER AND BLACK BEAN MARINATED
  SALMON WITH JASMINE RICE
CHILLED ZUCCHINI AND GREEN
  PEA SOUP

HERBED LAMB RACK OVER NEW
  POTATOES AND HONSHIMEJI
  MUSHROOMS
SPRING VEGETABLES AND ROASTED
  ARTICHOKE SAUCE

SALAD OF GREEN AND WHITE ASPARAGUS,
  OVEN DRIED TOMATOES AND YOUNG
  LETTUCES, TRUFFLE DRESSING

A BONSAI GARDEN OF SWEET SERENITY
ALMOND AND ORANGE MOUSSE CAKE
KIWI SAUCE

ST. CLEMENT *Chardonnay "Abbott's" 1997*
RIDGE *Cabernet Sauvignon "Monte Bello" 1991*
IRON HORSE *"Millennium Cuvée" 1994*

On one of her visits in the years prior to the Clinton administration, Queen Noor shares tea with Mrs. Reagan in the Red Room. Maitre d' Gene Allen presents them with pastries alongside a sugar basket filled with sugar violets.

PRESIDENT CLINTON IS ALLERGIC to chocolate, dairy products, and wheat, so I served a lot of frozen desserts to him and his guests during his administration. He especially loved mangoes and sour cherries, thus this ice cream mold, which I made for the dinner the Clintons hosted in the Blue Room for the king and queen of Jordan. The ice cream was decorated with pulled-sugar roses. The evening's *petit four* tray held a mixture of European and American treats, including hazelnut *soufflés*, pine nut cookies, cigarette cookies filled with *nougat*, and oatmeal *galettes*. I couldn't resist decorating each tray with pulled-sugar palm trees to honor the king.

The king and queen of Jordan were frequent guests at the White House. In previous years, when Queen Noor, wife of King Hussein, was in town, she dropped by the White House regularly for tea. It was always my pleasure to serve her. I never forgot that in 1983, shortly after I arrived at the White House, the manager of the palace called the kitchen directly (at first I thought it was a prank) and asked me to move to Jordan to be the palace pastry chef. It was a great honor, but I decided to see where the White House job would take me, and I never regretted that decision.

Mango and Sour Cherry Ice Cream Mold

Dinner, May 18, 1999

GRILLED DOVER SOLE
ASIAGO CHEESE RISOTTO
TOMATO FENNEL BROTH
CRISPY SAGE

CRUSTED LAMB LOIN
ROASTED GARLIC AND SHALLOTS
FRESH PORCINI MUSHROOMS,
  SUGAR SNAP PEAS, BABY CORN
NATURAL AU JUS

SPRING GREENS WITH ENDIVE
HAZELNUT DRESSING
BRIOCHE FILLED WITH GOAT CHEESE

MANGO AND SOUR CHERRY
  ICE CREAM MOLD
SUNRISE ORANGES, HAZELNUT SOUFFLÉ
PINE NUT COOKIES, OATMEAL GALETTE

CHALONE *Chardonnay 1997*

*Scandinavian dignitaries attended a reception celebrating the Viking exhibition at the
Smithsonian's National Museum of Natural History. King Harald V of Norway, with his wife Queen Sonja
next to him, speaks in the rotunda, where a large African bush elephant has greeted visitors since 1959.*

THE NATIONAL MUSEUM OF NATURAL HISTORY at the
Smithsonian Institution mounted a show entitled *Vikings:
The North Atlantic Saga* in April 2000. To celebrate its
opening, the White House hosted a luncheon, inviting "an
extraordinary assemblage of dignitaries from the Nordic
nations," their guests, and various supporters and staff at the museum. For
the occasion, many interesting artifacts from the show were temporarily displayed in the Cross Hall, the long corridor that runs from the State Dining
Room to the East Room.

There was no question about what I would make. It would have to be a
dessert served inside a Viking ship. In fact, I made fourteen ships out of
chocolate, and filled each one with lingonberry *sorbet* and vanilla ice cream,
covered with fluffy *meringue*. The ships were surrounded by thinly sliced
cantaloupe folded around sliced strawberries and set on kiwi sauce, to
resemble the waves of the sea. When the platters were brought in, people
burst into applause and took out their cameras. It was a break in decorum,
but not an unusual one during my tenure at the White House!

Lingonberry and Vanilla "Nordic Snow Drift"
with Anise Star Aquavit Sabayon and Warm Apricot Turnovers

Luncheon, April 28, 2000

CHILLED MOSAIC OF RED AND YELLOW
  TOMATO SOUP
GOAT CHEESE GÂTEAU
CUCUMBER AND BABY FENNEL SLAW

CHILEAN SEA BASS NIÇOISE
YOUNG FRENCH BEANS & ARTICHOKES
HERBED ANNA POTATOES
PICHOLINE OLIVE SAUCE

SALAD OF YOUNG GREENS AND PEA
  TENDRILS, HEARTS OF PALM AND
  ASPARAGUS SPEARS, CHAMPAGNE
  VINAIGRETTE

LINGONBERRY AND VANILLA
  NORDIC SNOW DRIFT
ANISE STAR AQUAVIT SABAYON
APRICOT TURNOVER

SHAFER *Chardonnay "Red Shoulder" 1997*

*President and Mrs. Clinton greet South African President Thabo Mbeki and
his wife Zanele at the North Portico prior to the start of the State Dinner.*

THERE IS SO MUCH INSPIRATION to be found in South Africa! For this dinner, I knew I wanted to use images of the beautiful animals of the plains. I just had to figure out how. Once I hit upon the idea of wrapping the images around a pineapple, it was full speed ahead.

Don't let the photo fool you. These desserts aren't real pineapples at all, but plum *sorbet* and pineapple Champagne *parfait*, sculpted and piped in the shape of beautiful, fresh fruit. I did want to finish each one with a real pineapple top. The difficulty was figuring out how to get the tops to stay in place and not tumble to the floor or onto someone's lap during service while the guests helped themselves to scoops of *sorbet* and *parfait*. It was an unwritten but very strict rule at the White House that accidents such as these not occur, at any cost.

This is how I was able to send the pineapples to the dining room with confidence. I made a chocolate plate, about 8 inches in diameter and 1 inch thick. I then attached a large chocolate dowel, 8 inches tall and 2 inches in diameter. To the top of this dowel I secured another chocolate disk, about 3 inches in diameter. I then molded the *sorbet* around the dowel and in between the chocolate disks in the shape of the pineapple. Using a large star tip, I piped the pineapple Champagne *parfait* over the plum *sorbet*, to resemble the pineapple skin. Finally, I glued the pineapple top to the smaller disk with some hard chocolate *ganache*, so it wouldn't slip off, even after all the frozen dessert was eaten.

After all of this, finishing the dessert was easy. I wrapped the white chocolate ribbon, printed with dark chocolate animals, around the dessert like a piece of film. Just before serving I arranged marinated fresh pineapple and some beautiful Queen Anne cherries around the dessert. A Tropico-flavored *sabayon* and *petits fours* decorated with *fondant*-dipped gooseberries were passed alongside the pineapples. All of these flavors worked amazingly well together, teaming up to make a dessert to remember.

The Pride of South Africa
Queenstown Pineapple Surprise with Tropico Sabayon and Gooseberries

Dinner, May 22, 2000

GREEN AND WHITE ASPARAGUS
WILD LEEK MARINATED LOBSTER
  MORELS AND TINY NEW POTATOES

APRICOT GINGER GLAZED LAMB
SAFFRON PISTACHIO COUSCOUS
HERBED SPRING VEGETABLES

SALAD OF YOUNG GREENS, ROASTED
  TOMATOES AND ARTICHOKES, GOAT
  CHEESE AND AVOCADO TERRINE,
  LEMON THYME DRESSING

THE PRIDE OF SOUTH AFRICA
QUEENSTOWN PINEAPPLE SURPRISE
TROPICO SABAYON
LINZER SQUARES, CAPE GOOSEBERRIES,
  COCONUT MACAROONS

LONG VINEYARD *Pinot Grigio 1999*
CHIMNEY ROCK *"Elevage" 1996*
S. ANDERSON *Blanc de Noirs 1995*

*President and Mrs. Clinton greet members of the band Earth, Wind and Fire
at the conclusion of their performance at the State Dinner for Morocco.*

SOMETIMES WHEN I WAS BRAINSTORM-ING a State Dinner dessert the idea came easily, but other times it seemed as though inspiration would never arrive. In the case of the dessert for the King Mohammed VI of Morocco, the latter was true. I wanted a dessert that communicated the idea of Morocco loud and clear, but after visiting every Moroccan restaurant in the Washington area, as well as paging through many picture-filled books about its art and architecture, talking to friends and colleagues who had been there, and even visiting the Moroccan Embassy, I was drawing a blank. I was worried. The dinner was to be held in an outdoor pavilion, which meant that logistically there would be limits on what I could serve. And it was a large dinner—350 guests. I'd need to make thirty-five desserts plus thirty-five bowls of dessert sauce and thirty-five trays of cookies, and as of two weeks before the dinner I had nothing.

But in my subconscious mind I must have been gathering ideas, because as I sat in a local coffee shop after work, doodling on my napkin, I suddenly had a vision of what the dessert would look like: a Moroccan oasis, covered with bright blue mosaic tiles. Once I had the image, the rest was easy. I would make dome-shaped cakes filled with *mousse*, reminiscent of Moroccan archi-tecture. I made arches out of chocolate to be placed on the sides of the structures to resemble the arched door-ways I saw in all of the pictures. The bright colors and beautiful mosaics led me to decorate my domes with vivid blue tiles made of colored chocolate. Around the perimeter of each cake I scattered orange segments and candied orange peels. I topped each large dome with a smaller dome made of ice cream and *sorbet*. I fashioned a background for each dome out of white *pastillage* and bent it so it looked like a movie screen. On the *pastillage* I painted some palm trees, a huge bright red sun, and a line of camels looking like they were receding into the desert. In the end the desserts, each serving ten people, looked like a marriage between Morocco and old Hollywood. I was delighted to hear on the morning after the dinner that the new king and President Clinton greatly admired my colorful set piece.

A Moroccan Oasis

Dinner, June 20, 2000

PEPPER SEARED SALMON
SALAD OF ARTICHOKES AND YOUNG
  VEGETABLES
GOLDEN TOMATO GAZPACHO
CHATEAU STE. MICHELLE *"Reserve"*
  Chardonnay 1997

LEMON GARLIC CRUSTED LAMB
BALSAMIC GLAZED VIDALIA ONIONS
CASSEROLE OF NEW POTATOES, FAVA
  BEANS AND CHANTERELLES

JUSTIN *"Isosceles" 1997*

WARM GOAT CHEESE TART
SPRING LETTUCE, CITRUS AND
  RADISHES, MISSION FIG DRESSING

"A MOROCCAN OASIS"
ORANGE AND DATE SWEET DELICACIES
HONEY MINT SAUCE, SESAME HONEY
  CAKES, ALMOND FILLED MEDJOOL
ARGYLE *"Julie Lee's Block" Blanc de Blancs 1996*

Each petit four tray is decorated with a white chocolate tiger and a chocolate tree.

WITH ROUGHLY EIGHT HUNDRED GUESTS, this was the largest State Dinner I ever catered. As the White House itself could not accommodate such a large number, the dinner was held in a tent outdoors. I decided on the lotus flower motif because it is so characteristically Indian. To construct the huge flowers, we first made a chocolate base and then attached pink chocolate petals to it. We made eighty lotus flowers, with a total of 3,500 petals! Then, we molded mango *sorbet* into the yellow pods that you see, filling each pod with a banana *mousse* mixed with crunchy pastry. The *petit four* trays, with honey-almond squares and chocolate-coconut bars, were each decorated with a white chocolate tiger whose stripes had been hand-painted with dark chocolate, and a dark chocolate tree. I wonder if anyone guessed that I had gone to the National Zoo and bought a plastic toy tiger to create the mold used for

this presentation! I know the tigers were appreciated because many of them were taken home as souvenirs.

All of the food was prepared in the residence and then transported to the South Lawn. The frozen dessert presented a challenge. When served, it had to be at just the right temperature—not rock solid, which would make it difficult to eat, but not soft to the point that the lotus would lose its shape. Compounding the difficulty were the number of desserts we had to serve and the fact that there was no freezer outdoors. On the day of the dinner, the pastry staff arranged the lychees and raspberries around the chocolate base, and just before serving we placed the mango and banana center on each one. Then the platters were carried to the pavilion, with the lotus softening to just the right consistency on the way there. As Fleetwood Mac played, none of the guests guessed how hard we worked to make and deliver this dessert without a hitch, which is exactly how I wanted it.

Mango and Banana Lotus
with Lychees and Raspberry Sauce

Dinner, September 17, 2000

DARJEELING TEA SMOKED POUSSIN
CHILLED GREEN PEA & CILANTRO SOUP
MARBLE POTATOES
WOLFFER VINEYARDS
 Chardonnay "Estate" 1997

WILD COPPER RIVER SALMON
RED KURI SQUASH, RICE BEAN RAGOÛT
SWISS CHARD CUSTARD
GARLIC–CHANTERELLE EMULSION
CALLAGHAN VINEYARDS
 "Buena Suerte Cuvee" 1997

YOUNG GREENS & HERB SALAD
HEIRLOOM TOMATOES
DRY AGED CHEESE BLOSSOM
25-YEAR OLD SHERRY DRESSING

MANGO & BANANA LOTUS
LYCHEES & RASPBERRY SAUCE
"A MAJESTIC TIGER'S DELIGHT"
HONEY ALMOND SQUARES
CHOCOLATE COCONUT BARS
TUALATIN ESTATE
 "Semi Sparkling" Muscat 1999

*President Bush presents Australian Prime Minister John Howard with the bell
from the World War II ship* Canberra *at the U.S. Navy Yard.*

*a*USTRALIA HAS A LOT TO OFFER in the way of inspiration
for the pastry artist. Every time I had to make a dessert for
an Australian event, I pictured the beautiful seashells, coral
reefs, and exotic fruits that are so bountiful there, and I
couldn't wait to replicate them in sugar.

I thought this dessert really evoked Australia. It was an oversized scallop shell made of puff pastry and filled with a light ginger custard cream
mixed with red currants, raspberries, strawberries, and pomegranate seeds. I
placed the top of the shell at a slight angle, so the scallop appeared to be
held open by the sliced strawberries. Lemon sauce decorated the platter,
with more served on the side. My favorite detail was the piece of blue sugar
coral, complete with some little puff pastry fish that I attached to the back
of the shell. After all of these years it's one of my favorite presentations.

Red Fruit and Ginger Cream
in a Puff Pastry Shell with Lemon Sauce

Luncheon, September 10, 2001

WARM SMOKED QUAIL
CORN AND FENNEL
PEACH AND BLACK WALNUT CHUTNEY

GRILLED BLOCK ISLAND SWORDFISH
SAFFRON MUSSEL SAUCE
OYSTER MUSHROOMS
NEW POTATOES

RADISH AND SPINACH SALAD
ENDIVE AND TOASTED GOAT CHEESE

RED FRUITS AND GINGER CREAM IN A
    PUFF PASTRY SEA SHELL
LEMON SAUCE

GEYSER PEAK *Chardonnay 1999*

Dessert was served on platters presented by Lenox to President and Mrs. George H. W. Bush to commemorate the 200th anniversary of the laying of the White House cornerstone. They were designed to supplement the Johnson china service, which First Lady Barbara Bush often used for State Dinners.

*E*VEN AFTER TWENTY YEARS at the White House, I viewed each assignment as a challenge and tried to come up with something original to honor each occasion. One of my favorite examples was made for the luncheon in honor of Lyudmila, the wife of Russian President Vladimir Putin. I wanted to create a ladylike dessert with the flavors favored in Russia.

When I visited Moscow in the late 1990s, I had observed the popularity of tea and honey, so I decided on a tea and honey ice cream. For the container, I used colored chocolate to reproduce the striped caviar tins I saw on my trip. The ice cream went in the tins, which I topped with chocolate "caviar." All that was needed was a lid, which I made with white chocolate and decorated with a beautiful flower, the petals made from pulled sugar and the center a blown-sugar ball. To finish things off, I offered warm caramel apples and lemon sauce for the ice cream along with cookies baked for the occasion.

One of the joys of serving dessert at the White House is the frequent opportunity to use many historic pieces of china from past administrations. I set these caviar tins on platters ordered by Barbara Bush for the White House.

Honey Tea Ice Cream
Topped with Chocolate Caviar

Luncheon, November 13, 2001

ARTICHOKE AND LEEK SOUP
NANTUCKET BAY SCALLOPS

PAN-SEARED POUSSIN
CORN AND MOREL MUSHROOM
  CUSTARD
GREEN BEANS AND PEARL ONIONS
TARRAGON-SCENTED AU JUS

AUTUMN GREENS
PEARS AND MAYTAG BLUE CHEESE
TOASTED WALNUTS
MUSTARD SHALLOT DRESSING

HONEY AND TEA ICE CREAM
CHOCOLATE CAVIAR
WARM CARAMEL APPLES
LEMON SAUCE

GARY FARRELL *Chardonnay "Russian River" 1999*

DINNER IN HONOR OF HER EXCELLENCY GLORIA MACAPAGAL-ARROYO, THE PRESIDENT OF THE REPUBLIC OF THE PHILIPPINES, AND ATTORNEY JOSE MIGUEL T. ARROYO

Arrangements for the State Dinner for the Philippines are previewed for the press in the State Dining Room. Left to right: Chef Walter Scheib, Florist Nancy Clarke, Assistant Chef Cris Comerford, Chief Usher Gary Walters, Assistant Pastry Chef Susan Morrison, and Pastry Chef Roland Mesnier.

For the State Dinner for the president of the Philippines, I wanted to create a dessert representing the friendship between the two countries. The *lei* as a symbol came to mind right away. To execute this idea, I made some very colorful sugar flowers and glued them to a chocolate base. Just before serving, the *leis* were draped over mango ice cream and coconut *mousse* molds, which were displayed on caramel and almond *nougat* stands. Alongside the frozen dessert, I served a warm baked pineapple topped with a crunchy sesame s*treusel* and honey *meringue*. The flavors were all a nod to Philippine favorites.

With this dessert, there could be no doubt that the president and first lady were honoring their guests.

Mango Coconut Lei
Baked Pineapple with Sesame Crumb

Dinner, May 19, 2003

MAINE DAYBOAT SCALLOPS

BRANDADE OF SMOKED TROUT AND
  MARYLAND CRABS

VINE-RIPENED TOMATO GAZPACHO

BELLEWETHER FARM LAMB

RED WINE REDUCTION

ACHIOTE POLENTA, FRESH FAVA BEANS,
  MORELS, AND BRAISED CIPOLLINI
  ONION

DU MOL *Pinot Noir "Finn" 2000*

AVOCADO, TOMATO, AND GOAT'S
  CHEESE TERRINE

SPRING GREENS

CANDIED PEPITAS CALAMANSI DRESSING

MANGO COCONUT LEI

BAKED PINEAPPLE WITH SESAME CRUMB

ASSORTED COOKIES

SCHRAMSBERG *Crémant 1999*

95

Giraffes made from blown sugar adorn each petit four tray in tribute to the abundant wildlife of Kenya.

IN 2002, FORMER PRESIDENT and Mrs. George H. W. Bush were received royally in Kenya by President Mwai Kibaki. Everyone who traveled with the Bushes came home raving about Kenyan hospitality. So in my mind we had to reciprocate and do even better the next year when President Kibaki visited us, during the George W. Bush administration.

I found it easy to be inspired by the task. First of all, I had always loved what grows abundantly in Kenya: coffee, pineapple, banana. Second, I had always been enchanted by the beauty of African wildlife. For that special night I wanted to honor both presidents, so I molded chocolate into the shape of an old-fashioned coffee grinder and decorated the grinder with a yellow rose of Texas made from sugar. Alongside the grinder I placed some coffee ice cream, molded to look like extra-large coffee beans. To intensify the coffee flavor and for textural contrast, each bean was filled with coffee liqueur *parfait*. Delicate white chocolate espresso cups adorned with a dark chocolate silhouette of a different African animal ringed the platter. Each cup was filled with a banana and tea *mousse*. Behind the coffee grinder I placed some caramelized bananas, and baked fresh pineapple was also passed with the dessert.

I didn't neglect the *petit four* tray. Decorating each platter of passion fruit *pâte de fruit*, coconut truffles, walnut *baklava*, and sesame macaroons was a blown-sugar giraffe that I had shaped freehand. That night we truly celebrated all of the flavors of Africa.

Best of Kenya

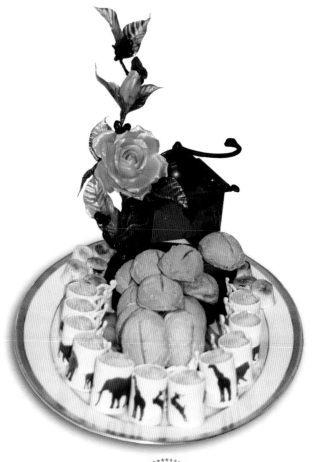

Dinner, October 6, 2003

ROASTED RACK OF LAMB
WILD MUSHROOMS AND ARMAGNAC
  SAUCE
SWEET POTATO FLAN
AUTUMN VEGETABLES

SOTER *Pinot Noir "Beacon Hill"*

AVOCADO AND HEIRLOOM TOMATO
  SALAD
TOASTED CUMIN DRESSING

"BEST OF KENYA"
ARABICA ICE CREAM AND COFFEE
  LIQUOR PARFAIT
CARAMELIZED BANANA AND PINEAPPLE

HONIG *Sauvignon Blanc "Late Harvest" 2002*

*The dessert for President Lula da Silva is an homage to the world's largest coffee producer, Brazil.
The petits fours continue the theme with a milk chocolate scoop filled with chocolate coffee beans.*

FOR THIS LUNCHEON honoring the president of Brazil, I naturally thought of coffee as my inspiration. Not only did I want to make a dessert layered with coffee flavor, but I wanted to design a presentation that said coffee, loud and clear. Wouldn't it be cool to mold coffee ice cream in the shape of a coffee pot? I did just that, and achieved just what I set out to do.

It really wasn't that difficult. I used a one-quart plastic container for the bottom part of the pot and a White House coffee cup to mold the top part. The handle, base, and spout were made of milk chocolate. To add some color, I placed a green sugar branch alongside the pot as a garnish.

To give the dessert an intensity of a strong cup of espresso, I made some coffee liqueur candies and stirred them into the ice cream. The candies, the size of large lima beans, had a very thin sugar crust and were filled with liqueur. When you took a bite of ice cream, you'd also break into a candy, which would release its ice-cold liqueur into your mouth. What an exquisite surprise! (Because President George W. did not drink alcohol, we omitted the candies from the dessert that went to his table.)

To surround each coffee pot, I made some white chocolate teacups and filled each one halfway to the top with a soft chocolate sauce. On top of the sauce was a portion of Tia Maria *parfait*. You can see that every cup was decorated with the presidential seal, in dark chocolate. The look of the tray was so elegant and the flavors so harmonious. *Petits fours* were designed with the look and taste of the dessert in mind: Tia Maria snaps, espresso caramel truffles, orange segments dipped in hard caramel, and a milk chocolate scoop filled with chocolate coffee beans.

Coffee Ice Cream Mold
with Tia Maria Parfait

Luncheon, June 20, 2003

SHRIMP AND CRAB GUMBO
STEAMED BASMATI RICE

THYME-SCENTED GRILLED LAMB CHOP
MADEIRA ESPANOLE SAUCE
CROQUETTE POTATOES
PEAS, ARTICHOKES AND BABY CARROTS

WATERCRESS AND BOSTON GREENS
WARM TEXAS GOAT CHEESE
WALNUT DRESSING

COFFEE ICE CREAM MOLD
TÍA MARIA PARFAIT
CHOCOLATE SAUCE

MAC ROSTIE *Chardonnay 2001*

SPECIAL EVENTS

President Bush presides over the Education Summit at the
University of Virginia in Charlottesville.

OCCASIONALLY, THE WHITE HOUSE kitchen staff caters an official event off-site, and for this Education Summit we traveled to Monticello, Thomas Jefferson's home in Charlottesville, Virginia. I was very excited to present a dessert at Monticello, knowing that Jefferson had been minister to France and brought his great love of French food and wine back with him to America. He even employed a French chief steward and a French chef at his home.

During the course of my research, I learned that Jefferson was particularly fond of pistachios, so I chose to make a very rich pistachio *marquise*, made with French butter and rich cream, just the kind of thing he would have enjoyed during his time in Paris. The *marquise* was layered with chocolate *joconde* and Parisian-style macaroons. Around the cake-shaped dessert I placed a chocolate fence similar to the fence surrounding Monticello. And at the head of each cake, I placed a piece of rock-sugar "limestone" topped with a chocolate bust of Jefferson. Autumn leaves made of sugar garnished the dessert, which rested in a pool of brilliant red raspberry sauce.

During my break, I had a chance to visit Jefferson's garden, in which I found all manner of fruits and vegetables. What a wonderful experience! Making the dessert, visiting Monticello, and touring Jefferson's beloved garden made me feel as if I had really communed with the great president and *gourmand*.

Pistachio Marquise
with Raspberry Sauce and Petits Fours

Dinner, September 27, 1989

TURBAN OF SEAFOOD MONTICELLO
AURORA SAUCE
SESAME SEED GALETTES

NOISETTES OF LAMB, MENTHE SAUCE
WILD MUSHROOM CROUSTADE
PARISIENNE POTATOES
VEGETABLE MEDLEY

SALAD OF GARDEN GREENS
BRIE CHEESE

PISTACHIO MARQUISE
RASPBERRY SAUCE
PETITS FOURS

MONTDOMAINE *Monticello Chardonnay 1986*
MONTICELLO *Pinot Noir 1987*
DOMAINE CHEURLIN *Brut*

*Petits fours designed in keeping with the "Fisherman's Fantasy" theme feature a red chocolate lobster
atop a white chocolate fishing net filled with chocolate fish and seashells.*

*a*LTHOUGH I OFTEN DESIGNED DESSERTS with specific
visual references to the event's honoree, every once in
a while I threw a curve ball, creating something entirely
whimsical and unexpected, just to get an amused and surprised reaction from the guests. I had been itching to do
this ocean-themed dessert for a while. The image of the lobster popped
into my head. From there, my imagination took over. When this event came
up on the schedule, I decided to go for it and make my "Fisherman's
Fantasy" a reality.

I made the lobster itself with watermelon *sorbet* and Grand Marnier
parfait (the tail) and red chocolate (the head, claw, and legs). I rested the
lobster on a bed of *nougat glacé* decorated with candied, glazed orange
segments, and poached lemon tartlets. The tartlets were topped with
candied lime peel that looked like seaweed.

As usual, I wanted the *petits fours* to relate to the dessert. So I made an
elevated white chocolate fishing net with a small red chocolate lobster. The
petits fours, along with some chocolate seashells and fish, looked like they
had been trapped in the net and were being pulled ashore.

Fisherman's Fantasy

Buffet Dinner, February 1, 1995

ORIENTAL VEGETABLE SALAD WITH SEARED
  SCALLOPS & TANGERINE VINAIGRETTE
GRILLED SHRIMP WITH RED POTATO
  AND WINTER VEGETABLE SALAD
RED CURRY & COCONUT DRESSING
PEPPERED TUNA WITH PAPAYA AND
  CUCUMBER SALAD
SMOKED CHICKEN & SOBA NOODLE
  SALAD WITH BLACK SESAME DRESSING
ARTICHOKE & ROASTED TOMATO SALAD
BARBECUED SEA BASS WITH AVOCADO

AND PEPPER RELISH
BAKED TROUT & LUMP CRABMEAT WITH
  ROASTED CORN AND SHERRY
ROASTED CHICKEN & VEGETABLE RAGOUT
CREOLE WHITE BEANS & GREENS
BUTTERNUT & BRUSSEL SPROUT SAUTE
BEEF TENDERLOIN WITH PROVOLONE &
  WILD MUSHROOM FILLING
PASTRY BUFFET
ADELSHEIM *Pinot Noir 1989*
KENWOOD *Chardonnay 1992*

*Pulled-sugar bees perch on the edge of silver bowls filled with honey sabayon. Petits fours
in the shape of acorns, mushrooms, and pumpkins continue the autumnal theme of the main dessert.*

THE DINNER RECOGNIZING THE RECIPIENTS of the National Medal of Arts and the National Medal of Humanities takes place every year in late September. At this time of year, the weather is still warm but not brutally so in Washington. The leaves start to display their brilliant colors. And of course the harvest arrives, with a bounty of autumn fruits.

Each component of my "Autumn Bounty" was inspired by the harvest and the season. The cranberry and Grand Marnier *terrine* was garnished with colorful frosted grapes. Wine-poached apples also garnished the platter. Brilliantly colored leaf-shaped cookies were arranged to look like they were ready to be raked into the chocolate container with the chocolate rake. On the side, I served honey *sabayon* in silver bowls, each bowl garnished by very realistic pulled-sugar bees. Even the cookie trays displayed my theme, with pumpkin- and mushroom- and acorn-shaped cookies.

Autumn Bounty

Dinner, September 29, 1997

CRISPY FILLET OF SEA BASS
RISOTTO OF ACORN SQUASH AND
 FINGERLING POTATO
KAFFIR INFUSED TOMATO BROTH

STUFFED PHEASANT
PINOT NOIR STEWED BLACK
 MISSION FIGS
LAYERED PORTOBELLO, BABY SPINACH
SAFFRON SCENTED AMARANTH
SAGE FRITTER

SALAD OF YOUNG HERBS AND MACHE
MAYTAG BLEU CHEESE SOUFFLÉ
ASIAN PEAR
PUMPKIN SEED OIL DRESSING

AUTUMN BOUNTY
PECAN AND PUMPKIN COOKIES

CLOS PEGASE *"Mitsuko Vineyard" Chardonnay 1995*
HESS COLLECTION *Cabernet Sauvignon 1992*
SCHRAMSBERG *"Cremant" 1992*

Baseball legends pose for a group photograph with President Bush in the East Room during the Baseball Hall of Fame luncheon.

*I*T IS WELL-KNOWN that President George W. Bush loves baseball. Before he was president, he was an owner of the Texas Rangers. At the White House he started a T-ball league, and games took place on Sundays on the South Lawn with up to forty boys and girls coming to play. As you can imagine, there were always many friends and family there to cheer on the children. The kitchen served hot dogs. For my part, I always prepared plenty of chocolate chip, peanut butter, and oatmeal cookies. And when I say plenty, I mean about 1600!

This is all to illustrate that baseball was a big deal at White House, never more so than the day of the Baseball Hall of Fame luncheon. I knew this event would require a bit more in the way of dessert than chocolate chip cookies. So I made chocolate cookie baseball gloves, holding *meringue* baseballs filled with *mousseline* and *mascarpone* passion fruit *mousse*. To make the gloves, I baked the cookies and then shaped them when they were still warm. After they cooled, I sprayed them with milk chocolate and piped the details with dark chocolate. The stitching on the *meringue* base-balls was piped with orange royal icing. A chocolate bat lay across each glove, and a strawberry *compote* accompanied the dessert. It was such a fun project, and fun to see everyone, especially the president, smile at the beautiful plates.

Play Ball!

Luncheon, March 30, 2001

FENNEL-CRUSTED SHRIMP
ROASTED ARTICHOKES AND TOMATOES
WILD SORREL SOUP

GRILLED VEAL PORTERHOUSE
GARLIC POLENTA
CHANTERELLES AND SPRING
  VEGETABLES

AVOCADO AND ORANGE SALAD
MEYER LEMON DRESSING

"PLAY BALL"
CHOCOLATE GLOVE
MERINGUE BALL WITH CHOCOLATE
  MOUSSELINE
MASCARPONE PASSION FRUITS

FESS PARKER *Chardonnay 1999*

Swans created with blown sugar accompany chocolate macaroons on the petit four trays.

THE GORGEOUS YELLOW OVAL ROOM, which sits directly over the Blue Room, is part of the first family's private quarters. From this room, you can access the Truman Balcony, which overlooks the pristine South Lawn, with the Ellipse and Washington Monument in the background. It is a special spot for first families to enjoy, but rarely used for entertaining. But on the occasion of the luncheon for the governors' spouses in 2002, First Lady Laura Bush wanted to share the lovely room and its view with her guests.

The elegant room called for a light dessert with a refined look. I layered strawberry ice cream and lemon *parfait* (an airy frozen *mousse*) with paper-thin pieces of *nougat* and crushed lemon macaroons in round molds. Each dessert was covered in a sugar cage, spun to look the like the wisteria that covered the staircase on the south side of the mansion. Completing the presentation was "Swan Lake": *pâte à choux* swans floating on a light lime cream surrounding each cage. A single swan topped each cage. Guests were instructed to lightly tap on the cages, which would shatter, so they could access the frozen dessert inside.

Very often when I served an elaborately decorated dessert, I prepared *petit four* or cookie trays to match. In this case, I set out platters of chocolate macaroons, each one decorated with swans and other pond creatures made of blown sugar. The photo here shows one tray with two blown-sugar swans on a sugar lake with cattail in the background.

Strawberry and Lemon Sorbet
Under a Wisteria Sugar Cage on Swan Lake

Luncheon, February 25, 2002

ENGLISH PEA SOUP
QUAIL EGGS BENEDICT
BRIOCHE CROUTON

VANILLA-SCENTED MAINE LOBSTER
WARM VEGETABLE SLAW
SILVER CORN-GOAT CHEESE FLAN
CITRUS VINAIGRETTE

STRAWBERRY AND LEMON SORBET
  UNDER A WISTERIA SUGAR CAGE ON
  SWAN LAKE
CHOCOLATE MACAROONS

MAC ROSTIE *Chardonnay 1999*

President Bush addresses the National Governors Association in the State Dining Room during its annual meeting in Washington, D.C.

THE GOVERNORS' DINNER is an annual White House event. That means I made two dozen Governors' Dinner desserts, every year something new. In 2003 I wanted to do something especially fun and entertaining, something that the Republican and Democratic governors could enjoy together, and this is what I came up with.

I called the dessert "An American Dream," and the joke was that some day the opposing parties could get along. For each tray I made a blown-sugar donkey and elephant, exactly the same size for the sake of equality. I faced them toward each other, just the way the dinner guests would face each other at the table. A round sugar platter rested on their outstretched legs. Miniature key lime pies and strawberries surrounded them. Alternating columns of raspberry, blueberry, and coconut sat on top of the tray. And towering above everything was an ice cream eagle.

During dinner, the atmosphere in the dining room was rather subdued. But when the butlers returned to the kitchen after serving the dessert, they reported that the crowd had erupted into animated chatter and roars of laughter. What was going on? One of the butlers who had been present just said, "You should see what they've done to your donkeys and elephants!" When the platters were returned to the kitchen, the *sorbet,* ice cream, and key lime pies were gone. The donkeys and elephants? They had all been decapitated by the dinner guests! My sugar pieces had done the job—giving Republicans and Democrats an opportunity to have a good time together around the table! I couldn't have been more delighted with this achievement in diplomacy.

An American Dream

Dinner, February 23, 2003

SEARED DIVER SCALLOP
MARINATED ARTICHOKES AND
  HEIRLOOM TOMATOES
TARRAGON SHALLOT SAUCE

WOLFFER ESTATE *Chardonnay "Reserve" 2000*

ROSEMARY-GARLIC VEAL ROAST
CONFIT OF ROOT VEGETABLES
WHIPPED YUKON GOLD POTATOES
CABERNET SAUCE

BECKER *Cabernet "Reserve" 2001*

MAYTAG BLUE CHEESE TART
BRAISED PEAR AND WINTER GREENS
SHERRY DRESSING

"AN AMERICAN DREAM"
BLUEBERRY AND RASPBERRY SHERBET
COCONUT ICE CREAM
KEY LIME PIE

DOMAINE MERRIWETHER *"Discovery Cuvée"*

The United States flag flies over the North Portico of the White House.

FOR THIS LUNCHEON, all the military brass were at the White House. The setting was formal, with flags hanging all around room. It was impressive to see so many decorated generals and other officers in military dress. I wanted a patriotic dessert that celebrated these heroes. So I wrapped ice cream and *sorbet* cakes with dark chocolate ribbon and then decorated that ribbon with a white chocolate ribbon imprinted with tiny American flags. Gold chocolate stars were attached to the wider ribbon. An eagle made of lemon *sorbet* topped each cake. Fresh figs and melon set on top of raspberry sauce provided a fresh fruit garnish.

An incident a few weeks after the luncheon added an amusing footnote to the luncheon. A leak damaged the beautiful ceiling in the State Dining Room. The White House painters were able to repair all but four of the many plaster stars above President Abraham Lincoln's portrait, which hung over the marble mantel. I happened to overhear my friends the painters despairing over how to replace these stars and was reminded of the silicone mold I made for the chocolate stars that decorated the dessert for this luncheon. My chocolate stars were replicas of the ones on the ceiling. I assured them that I could produce what they needed, but I don't think they believed me until I showed up in the dining room the next day with twelve beautiful stars made of plaster of Paris. I'm proud to say that not only did I leave my mark as White House pastry chef, but I contributed four stars to the ceiling of the White House State Dining Room, making me part of the building forever.

Ice Cream and Sorbet Cake

Luncheon, July 14, 2003

CHILLED SWEET POTATO SOUP WITH
  SMOKED QUAIL
TOASTED PASTA PEARLS

ROASTED LOIN OF SWORDFISH WITH
  LEMON AND ROSEMARY
SUMMER VEGETABLES AND CRISPY
  POLENTA
CIPPOLINI ONION AND CHANTERELLE
  SAUCE

ORANGE JICAMA AND AVOCADO SALAD
  WITH CILANTRO DRESSING

CANTALOUPE AND PORT WINE FROZEN
  MOUSSE
ASSORTED MELONS AND MISSION FIGS
COOKIES

MARTIN RAY *"Mariage" Chardonnay 2000*

The press reports from Pebble Beach, just off the North Lawn of the White House, early in the George W. Bush administration.

*a*T ONE TIME OR ANOTHER, most of the presidents I served invited high-level correspondents to the White House for a meal. I always wondered if these tough-talking reporters might not be a bit uncomfortable around the table with the president after critiquing his performance on television throughout the year. The dessert I created for this luncheon was intended to foster an atmosphere of *détente* and relaxation. The cake was a coconut *dacquoise*, filled with very light coconut buttercream and chocolate *mousseline*. The old-fashioned television set, complete with rabbit ear antennae, was molded from a thick piece of chocolate. Ripe raspberries, blueberries, and blackberries completed the presentation. Mangoes in apricot Grand Marnier sauce were passed as an accompaniment.

"Reporting from Around the World" Cake

Luncheon, January 20, 2004

WILD MUSHROOM SOUP
ROCK SHRIMP
BASIL OIL

GRILLED LAMB CHOPS
JALAPENO MINT SAUCE
ARTICHOKE, BRAISED ENDIVE, AND
  BABY CARROTS
POTATO-CHIVE PUREE

MESCULIN GREENS

ROASTED PEPPER, OLIVES, AND FETA
  CHEESE
SHALLOT DRESSING

"FROM AROUND THE WORLD"
COCONUT AND CHOCOLATE MOUSSE
  CAKE WITH SWEET RIPE MANGO

SHAFER *Chardonnay "Red Shoulder" 2001*

FAMILY CELEBRATIONS

Easter Treats for Amy Carter

WHEN I STARTED MY JOB at the White House in 1980, the Carter family had been there for three years and had been through three pastry chefs. I was so proud to be in the mansion on Pennsylvania Avenue, and also a little bit worried about succeeding where others had failed. But the Carter family, especially the children, first daughter Amy and grandson James III (son of Chip and Caron Carter), quickly put me at ease.

Amy had a passion for roller-skating that once got her in hot water with the press, when it was reported that she used the East Room as a roller rink. What was not reported was her love of cookie baking while roller-skating! She had a habit of calling for sugar cookie ingredients to be delivered to the first family's kitchen so she could make cookies for her school friends. Then she'd make the dough, put her cookies in the oven, and forget all about them while she took off on her roller-skates. The Secret Service would have to run into the family's kitchen to pull the burning cookies from the oven. The next morning, sheepish Amy would show up in my kitchen, where I always had some cookies stashed away for her to take to her classmates.

Who wouldn't love to make treats for such a fun-loving child? In this photo, I'm with Amy and James III, looking at an Easter display made with chocolate and *marzipan*. One of my most treasured documents from that time: a handwritten copy of Amy's very own sugar cookie recipe.

April 6, 1980

Mother's Day Party

I WAS SO TOUCHED when Mrs. Carter asked me to make a big, beautiful Mother's Day cake—not for her, but for the military wives' get-together at Andrews Air Force Base.

I decided on a huge strawberry cake, perfect for the season. It would be heart-shaped, to express love, and be decorated with the most pretty, old-fashioned icing roses. To top it off, I made some lovely blown-sugar swans and a heart-shaped *pastillage* box, upon which a sugar butterfly had alighted.

May 11, 1980

JIMMY CARTER ADMINISTRATION

121

President Carter's 56th Birthday

MY MIND REELED when I got this assignment in late September 1980—my very first birthday cake for the president of the United States. I was so honored. I'll remember this cake always.

From the start, one of my favorite jobs was making desserts for private first family celebrations. For this one, I was told that there would be no big party; the Democratic National Convention was just days after President Carter's birthday. But this didn't mean I was not going to go full-out to make the most exciting cake I could. The flavors were two of my favorites, chocolate and praline. The cake was covered with pristine white *fondant* and decorated with a piped chocolate inscription and border. To make it really special during the election season, I crafted an additional decoration: a blown-sugar donkey, pulling a sugar wagon loaded with white sugar carnations.

Shortly after the convention, Mrs. Carter came to the kitchen to tell me how much everyone had enjoyed the cake. The Carters had even taken the leftovers, along with the donkey, to the convention to share with friends! I was so pleased, and it gave me the confidence I needed to make many more birthday cakes for future first families.

October 1, 1980

JIMMY CARTER ADMINISTRATION

President and Mrs. Cleveland's Wedding Cake

WHEN I ARRIVED at the White House, I very much looked forward to contributing a cake to a grand White House wedding. Although I made cakes for the small weddings of presidents' relatives, I regret that I never got to make a huge, show-stopping cake for a bigger event.

Well, not exactly. In August 1987, a filmmaker requested that I re-create President Grover Cleveland's wedding cake for a documentary. The public was fascinated with his 21-year-old bride, Frances Folsom, who became the most popular first lady since Dolley Madison. My cake, replicated from a drawing, was 5 feet tall with decorations of royal icing and *pastillage* that I created freehand, including the wedding couple carved in sugar.

The long veil of the bride cascaded down the cake. I placed a family crest with the initials *GF* in front of the couple, and alongside a delicate sugar basket filled with light pink sugar roses and two white sugar doves. On the tier below, I filled a horn of plenty with tiny fruits and flowers of icing sugar. Below that gilded sugar oak leaves framed "1886," the year of the wedding. The tier itself looked like a drum, with sugar tassels and French horns all around. Supporting these tiers was the largest cake layer, decorated to resemble the underskirt of a wedding dress. On the base was a replica of the church the Clevelands attended and a church book engraved with their names.

Alas, my cake never got the close-up it deserved. As I was making the finishing touches, I was informed that the film had been canceled.

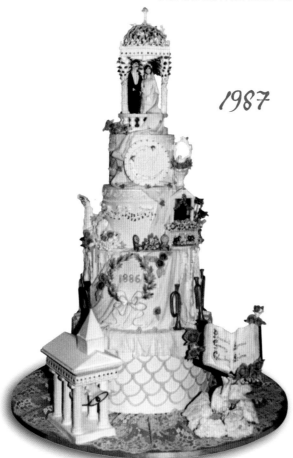

1987

Bush Family Christmas

WHEN PRESIDENT GEORGE H. W. BUSH and First Lady Barbara Bush moved into the White House, it was all about Millie. I suspected she was a very special dog, and this was confirmed when she wrote a best-selling book. Then she blessed the White House with six puppies. What a sight it was to see those little doggies running on the South Lawn with the president watching over them. I must confess that I could never resist sneaking up to first ladies' beauty parlor on the Second Floor, where the puppies were kept, when I knew the coast was clear. I loved to play with them. They were so precious and funny and full of life.

Millie herself was often an inspiration to me. I painted her with food coloring on sugar and surrounded the painting with pulled-sugar autumn leaves, pulled-sugar cattails, and a blown-sugar squirrel. I didn't forget the "Beware of Dog" sign, similar to ones President Reagan had placed on the lawn near the Oval Office in earlier years to tease his vice president about Millie's love of chasing squirrels. He said he placed the signs low to the ground so the poor squirrels would be able to read them.

For a Christmas brunch for family and friends in 1990, I wanted to make a centerpiece to delight everyone. So I made Millie in blown-sugar, dressed as Santa, driving a sleigh filled with sweet gifts pulled by four blown-sugar reindeer. It was one of the most light-hearted and fun pieces I did during my years at the White House. The children appreciated it almost as much as Mrs. Bush did!

December 25, 1990

Easter During the Clinton Years

E ASTER WAS ALWAYS ONE OF MY favorite holidays at the White House, and never more so than during the Clinton years. President and Mrs. Clinton's appreciation of my work gave me incentive to try harder to impress them as the years went by.

Easter motifs lend themselves to beautiful pastry- and candy-making. I always made a huge showpiece of a chocolate egg (or sometimes a bunny), every year decorating it in a new way.

Perhaps my favorite Clinton Easter egg is the one dominated by a white sugar peacock. The royal icing daffodils celebrating spring decorate the base, which is topped with blown-sugar eggs. The body of the peacock was made of blown sugar. I made each pulled sugar feather on its body individually—a long and tedious process but well worth the result. The photo also displays work of the wonderful White House Flower Shop.

1993 – 2000

WILLIAM J. CLINTON ADMINISTRATION

Chelsea Clinton's Birthdays

<hr>

I HAD THE HONOR and the pleasure of making quite a few birthday cakes for Chelsea Clinton, and it was so much fun to come up with something different for her every year. For her 14th birthday, I made a cake decorated with blown-sugar ballet shoes hanging by delicate sugar ribbons from a sugar rosebush (see page 118). When I brought the cake into the dining room filled with some very excited young people, I was impressed to see that the official photographer for the event was the president himself. He joked, "You know, Roland, I can take care of Bosnia no problem, but Chelsea and her friends are a handful!"

For Chelsea's 15th birthday, Mrs. Clinton asked me to make a cake in the shape of a milestone, with the number 15 on it. Because Chelsea enjoyed hiking, I made the cake look like a tree stump milestone found on hiking trails. The rucksack was made of sugar. The birds, apples, pears, and peaches surrounding it were molded from *sorbet*.

The next year was Chelsea's Sweet Sixteen. I wanted to make a cake that she would remember, not just something frosted with a few flowers on top. I had heard on the news that Chelsea had told her father she wanted a car and a driver's license for her birthday. I didn't know if the Clintons would deliver, but I sure would. I made a chocolate car—a souped-up Jeep—to place on top of a strip of pavement made from chocolate covered crisped rice wafers, which in turn was placed on top of the cake. The jeep's license plate read "Sweet 16," of course. Some sugar ballet shoes (recalling the ones from the earlier cake) hung from the jeep's rearview mirror. In addition, I made a hand-painted sugar driver's license, complete with a picture of Chelsea, inside a sugar envelope. We had the cake carefully transported to Camp David, where she celebrated the big day with her friends and family.

February 27, 1994

Godfrey Sperling's Breakfast Birthday Cake

L ONGTIME *CHRISTIAN SCIENCE MONITOR* COLUMNIST Godfrey Sperling was also the founder of the Washington, D.C., ritual known as the Sperling Breakfast. Beginning in 1966 and continuing until his retirement, he gathered select journalists several times a month to talk with politicians. Over the years, many headline-making stories were conceived over coffee and bacon and eggs as the writers questioned guests in this informal but influential forum.

President Clinton, whose own turn as a Sperling Breakfast guest proved pivotal to his election, invited Mr. Sperling to host the breakfast at the White House on his 80th birthday. This is the cake I designed especially for the occasion: everything, including the "tablecloth," was made of sugar or chocolate. The scrambled eggs are made of *crème brûlée*. The coffee is corn syrup, which I chose because it wouldn't spill as I rolled the cake into the dining room. I molded the bacon from *marzipan* and I made the flower centerpiece of pulled sugar. Since Mr. Sperling always had his newspaper with him at the table, I included a pulled-sugar copy at his place setting. The cake itself was a dairy-free carrot cake, a Clinton White House favorite

Believing that I had thought of every detail, I was excited to present this cake to the president's honored guest. But you can't anticipate everything. My assistants and I wheeled the cake, atop a metal cart, into the State Dining Room with no problem. But when we lifted the cart over the edge of the thick dining room carpeting, one of the wheels fell off. In front of everyone, I had to get down on my hands and knees to screw it back on before proceeding, as if nothing had happened, to the center of the room. The interruption lent a few extra moments of suspense to the ultimate presentation, which was all the more gratifying to me because of this minor glitch.

October 2, 1995

Mrs. Clinton's 50th Birthday

WHEN FIRST LADY Hillary Clinton turned 50, it was national news— *Time* magazine even put her on its cover, as a representative of women baby boomers reaching a milestone. Mrs. Clinton is all about achievements, so I wanted to celebrate some of them with a mocha walnut cake, her favorite.

Because she had just supervised the refurbishment of the White House Blue Room, I chose blue and white for the colors of the cake. The base is a reproduction of the Blue Room rug. She had also just published her book, *It Takes a Village*. I reproduced the book in *pastillage*, hand-painting the cover with food coloring. Beside the book, I placed what I call my Hillary Clinton Rose, a beautifully complex sugar flower I created especially for her and often made on occasions such as this one.

Hovering over the cake were life-sized blown sugar balloons. These were my achievement. Making them was similar to blowing glass. First I cooked some sugar, water, lemon juice, and corn syrup to a light caramel. Then I poured the caramel onto a slab of oiled marble to cool enough so it was workable. I dropped food coloring on top of the liquid caramel and then began pulling it until it became opaque and shiny, working under a heat lamp so the sugar remained soft enough to work with. Once it was ready, I placed a ball of the hot sugar at the end of a tube the size of a drinking straw and blew hot air into the tube, shaping the sugar into a ball. Each balloon was set aside to cool completely before it was attached to the cake. Getting the balloons to appear to float over the cake was another challenge!

The birthday party was held in an outdoor pavilion on the White House lawn on a brilliantly sunny day in the fall. As I had hoped, the cake brought a big smile to her face.

October 26, 1997

Marshall Bush's Sweet Sixteen Cake

THE BUSH FAMILY loved to get together, and the occasion of Marshall Bush's Sweet Sixteen was no exception. Marshall, the niece of George W. Bush, was a familiar face at the mansion during both Bush administrations. I was determined to make a cake just for her, so she would remember it always. I got my hands on a photo of her family pets—two adorable dogs, one white and one black—and reproduced them in chocolate so they could sit atop her cake. I didn't stop there. Two pink chocolate hearts were inscribed with "Marshall," and "Happy Sweet 16." Pulled-sugar roses and a white and pink sugar ribbon added feminine touches that I hoped the teenager would like. And, of course, there were sixteen candles for the birthday girl.

It was a wonderful evening, and I got a big hug from Marshall in thanks for the "masterpiece." I asked her if she remembered her first White House birthday party, when she turned 3 and her grandmother, First Lady Barbara Bush, was the host. Here we were, thirteen years later! I truly loved this part of my job, making special desserts for some of the children I had a chance to see growing up. I received a nice note from Marshall's father, Marvin Bush, almost a year after the party. There was no breach of manners—at the time of the party, all mail sent to the White House kitchen was considered undeliverable for many months because of the ongoing anthrax investigation!

May 15, 2002

GEORGE W. BUSH ADMINISTRATION

GINGERBREAD HOUSES

*a*LTHOUGH I LIKE TO THINK my claim to fame is that in my twenty-five years as White House pastry chef I never served the same dessert twice, I realize I am better known for the elaborate gingerbread houses I crafted for the Christmas holidays. If you've ever made a gingerbread house of your own, you know how it generates wonderful memories. Here are some of my favorites.

I built my first gingerbread house in 1992. I called it "Santa's Village," and it included sledding elves, reindeer, and Barbara Bush in her famous pearls, bringing cookies to Santa. Mrs. Bush loved it!

In 1993, the Clintons' first year in the White House, I made a gingerbread White House for the first time. I called it, "The Home of Socks" (the Clintons' cat). I placed more than twenty miniature *marzipan* Sockses in the rooms of the house, which was built to scale and adorned with chocolate trees and other decorations copied from the traditional White House decor. Spotlights illuminated the house at night.

In 1994, I made a replica of President Clinton's childhood home in Hope, Arkansas. It was such a success that in 1995 I made Mrs. Clinton's

childhood home in Chicago. Peeking into the house, you could see two of its completely furnished rooms, with working lights. In one of the rooms was a *marzipan* young lady tucked into bed, dreaming of sugar plums. In 1996 I celebrated Chelsea's love of dance with a beautiful house flanked by two nutcrackers. All the characters from *The Nutcracker Suite*, made of icing, were inside, including Chelsea as the Sugar Plum Fairy in a pink ballerina dress. In 1997, I went back to Santa's workshop, updating it by placing Santa in his sleigh outside, with a cell phone in his hand! The press loved this one, and dozens of newspapers around the country ran a photo of the modern Santa.

Beginning in 1998, the gingerbread house was displayed in the State Dining Room every year, and I worked to make each one bigger and more spectacular than the last. For 1998 I built a huge castle, with skating ponds on either side. Socks skated atop one, and Buddy, the Clintons' new Labrador retriever, twirled on the other. For the Millennium, Mrs. Clinton asked me to re-create in gingerbread four of the most recognizable buildings around Washington. I chose the Jefferson Memorial, the first White

House (before the 1814 fire), Mount Vernon, and the Washington Monument, all built to scale. For their last Christmas in the White House, in 2000, Mrs. Clinton wanted another replica of what had become their home. This time I opened up three rooms for viewing: the Blue Room had Christmas trees, Santa, and guests; the State Dining Room had a Christmas buffet with all sorts of goodies, a fireplace, and a working chandelier; and the East Room had many festive decorations.

The gingerbread tradition continued with the next administration. For their first White House Christmas, Laura Bush wanted a historical gingerbread White House, so I built mine to look like the mansion in John Adams's time, before the Truman Balcony was built. I filled the portico with carolers and the White House pets, Spot and Barney. On top was an angel, just as Mrs. Bush had requested. Pets always proved popular, so in 2002 I made a gingerbread house decorated with all the presidents' pets, including John Quincy Adams's alligator, Woodrow Wilson's sheep, and Theodore Roosevelt's ponies and roosters.

To draw attention to Mrs. Bush's literacy initiative, the next year's house was populated by characters from many children's books, including her favorite, *Good Night Moon*. My last gingerbread house, in 2006, had an enchanting color scheme of red and white. I covered it with 800 sugar snowflakes and decorated a huge Christmas tree up front with red and white sugar Christmas balls.

These houses were enormous undertakings, and I couldn't have constructed them without the help of everyone working in the pastry kitchen during the holiday rush. But there was another set of White House elves who contributed advice and crucial equipment every year: the workers in the Carpentry Shop were always ready with ideas, band saws, files, and other tools that they used for household repairs.

GLOSSARY OF PASTRY TERMS

amaretto an Italian macaroon made with bitter almond

baklava a Greek dessert made of thin sheets of *phyllo* dough with layers of finely chopped nuts and honey, soaked in syrup

barquette a boat-shaped pastry shell filled with fruit or custard

blown sugar pulled sugar that is made into thin-walled, hollow shapes by being blown up like a balloon

brioche a light, slightly sweet bread made with a rich yeast dough containing eggs and butter

buttercream an icing made with butter blended with confectioners' sugar or sugar syrup

caramelize to brown sugar by heating it, sometimes with fruits or nuts

charlotte a dessert made of cream or *mousse* and spices in a special mold lined with *ladyfingers*

compote a dessert of fruit cooked in a sugar syrup

cream puff a round, light pastry with a whipped cream filling

crème brûlée (literally, "burnt cream") a dessert consisting of a rich custard base topped with a hard layer of caramelized sugar

croquembouche a high cone of caramel-coated cream puffs decorated with caramel threads, sugared almonds, chocolate flowers, or ribbons

dacquoise a light, crisp *meringue* made with ground nuts, often layered with buttercream

décor chocolate chocolate of a consistency that can be used for piping or decorating

dulce de leche a thick, caramel-based sauce

flambé to douse with liquor (brandy, rum, or cognac) and ignite

fondant a soft, creamy preparation of sugar, water, and flavoring that is boiled and rolled into a shiny white paste, used as a basis for candies or icings

galette a freeform pastry filled with fruits and baked

ganache a sweet, creamy mixture of chocolate and whipping cream used as a filling or frosting

génoise a sponge cake containing butter, sugar, and stiffly beaten eggs

gianduja a sweet chocolate containing hazelnut paste

glacé iced, or finished with a smooth, glossy surface

glaze a shiny coating

infusion oil or water that has been flavored with herbs or berries

joconde an almond sponge cake

kourabiede a Greek crescent-shaped butter cookie made with almonds

ladyfinger a small, dry, finger-shaped sponge cake or cookie

macaroon a small sandwich cookie composed chiefly of egg whites, sugar, and ground almonds or coconut, with a filling

marquise a form of cake icing

marzipan a combination of almond paste, sugar, and corn syrup, used as an icing, for decorative work, or for molding candies and figures

mascarpone an Italian cream cheese

meringue a dessert topping consisting of a baked mixture of stiffly beaten egg whites and sugar, or a shell made of *meringue* that is filled with fruit or ice cream

mousse (literally, "foam"): a light, spongy dessert containing eggs, flour, and whipped cream, bound with gelatin, or a molded chilled dessert made with sweetened and flavored whipped cream or egg whites and gelatin

mousseline buttercream lightened with *meringue*, used as a filling for cakes and pastries

nougat a confection of nut or fruit pieces in a sugar paste

parfait a flavored custard containing whipped cream and syrup frozen without stirring, or a cold dessert made of layers of fruit, syrup, ice cream, and whipped cream

pastillage a sugar paste, used for decorative work, that becomes very hard when dry

pâte à choux cream puff pastry

pâte de fruit a bite-size fruit jelly covered in crystallized sugar

petit four a small cake cut from a pound or sponge cake and frosted, often layered and decorated, designed as an individual dessert to be eaten in one or two bites

phyllo a paper-thin dough or pastry

pipe to force icing or chocolate through a tube for decorating

pulled sugar sugar that is boiled to the hard-crack stage, allowed to harden, and then pulled or stretched until it develops a pearly sheen

purée a paste or liquid thick suspension made from cooked fruit ground very finely or forced through a sieve

royal icing icing made of confectioners' sugar and egg whites, used for decorating

sabayon a foamy dessert or sauce made of egg yolks whipped with wine or liqueur, served over fruit

sfogliatelle an Italian shell-shaped pastry, light and flaky, filled with ricotta or almond paste

sorbet a fruit-flavored ice served as a dessert

soufflé a feather-light baked dessert made mostly of beaten eggs or egg whites alone, with a sauce or flavoring, baked until fluffed up

sous chef assistant chef

sponge cake a light, airy cake made by whipping eggs and sugar to a foam, then folding in flour

spun sugar boiled sugar made into long, thin threads by dipping wires into the sugar syrup and waving them so that the sugar falls off in fine streams

streusel a crumbly mixture of butter, sugar, and flour, and sometimes chopped nuts, oats, and spices, that is used as a topping or filling for a cake

terrine a square or oval mold

tiramisu an Italian dessert made with layers of sponge cake or *ladyfingers, mascarpone,* and espresso, dusted with cocoa or shaved chocolate

tuile a thin, crisp, sweet cookie with a curved shape

zeppola an Italian deep-fried dough ball made of flour, white sugar, and almonds

INDEX

ILLUSTRATION CREDITS

All images are in the collection of Roland Mesnier and copyrighted by the White House Historical Association unless listed below.

ACKNOWLEDGMENTS

I would like to give a big thank you to all the people at the White House for the help and assistance they gave me during my twenty-five years as pastry chef, and especially to those in the Usher's Office, the Photo Office, the Office of the Curator, the Flower Shop, the Carpentry Shop, and the Electric Shop, and to the butlers, the calligraphers, the engineers, and those who worked in housekeeping, store room, and operations, and of course my great assistant Susan Morrison, and all my wonderful pastry staff. I would also like to thank Lauren Chattman for helping me write this book, and Neil Horstman and the staff of the White House Historical Association for supporting and producing this book.—Roland Mesnier